THE
MAXIMS
OF
GENERAL
PATTON

THE
MAXIMS
OF
GENERAL
PATTON

Gary L. Bloomfield

PELICAN PUBLISHING COMPANY
Gretna 2013

To my father, Army Command Sgt. Maj. Robert D. Bloomfield, who taught me to never give in, to never back down, to never give up, and to never ever quit. His hero was General Patton.

The word "Pelican" and the depiction of a pelican are trademarks of Pelican Publishing Company, Inc., and are registered in the U.S. Patent and Trademark Office.

Library of Congress Cataloging-in-Publication Data

Bloomfield, Gary L.
  The maxims of General Patton / by Gary L. Bloomfield.
    p. cm.
  Includes bibliographical references.
  ISBN 978-1-4556-1724-1 (pbk : alk. paper) – ISBN 978-1-4556-1725-8 (e-book) 1. Patton, George S. (George Smith), 1885-1945–Quotations. 2. Quotations, American. I. Patton, George S. (George Smith), 1885-1945. II. Title.
  E745.P3B53 2012
  355.0092–dc23
  [B]
                                        2012018787

Printed in the United States of America
Published by Pelican Publishing Company, Inc.
1000 Burmaster Street, Gretna, Louisiana 70053

Contents

Acknowledgments

This book could not have been completed without the invaluable assistance of numerous agencies, over the course of many years:

The editors, researchers, and historians at the U.S. Army Combined Arms Center at Fort Leavenworth, and especially the staff at *Military Review,* who provided access to their archives, including official documents, speeches, unit histories, maps, and photos.

The General George Patton Museum of Leadership at Fort Knox, just south of Louisville. I spent countless hours digging through their archives, long before they were made available online. Thank you for showing me little-known treasures from your vast collection and for allowing me access to your library and archives. Also thank you for providing many of the photos used in this book.

The Library of Congress and National Archives in Washington, D.C. Long before the Internet, I spent many hours researching files and photos there (first as managing editor of *VFW* magazine, then for several World War II books, including this one).

West Point. When I was seven, my father took me there

on our way to visit relatives in Toronto. At the Military Academy, we stopped by the statue of Gen. George Patton, my father's boyhood hero. From my small vantage point, he looked massive, larger than life, and after hearing my father's stories about America's most notorious World War II leader, I understood why he was invincible. Many years later, as managing editor of *VFW,* I relied on the staff at West Point for photos, paintings, and reference documents, and I continue to do so for my books. Thank you, to everyone, for your guidance and patience.

The Public Affairs Office at Fort Riley, Kansas. Having served two tours there with the Big Red One (the First Infantry Division, which had a red *1* on its shoulder patches), I was able to research General Patton and his impact on early army training and tactics. This was long before I ever considered writing a book about Patton. Fortunately I'm a packrat and kept all of the reference files for more than twenty years before using them for this book.

The Public Affairs Office and the Command Historian for U.S. Army Europe in Heidelberg, Germany. This was another duty assignment, where I took advantage of access to references not available to the general public and began compiling my own files and photos of the army's history in World War II, a history in which General Patton played a prominent role.

Introduction

George Patton was born to be a warrior. As a boy, he had heard the tales and read with wonder the stories of adventure and conquest, of heroes returning home to rousing ovations, of fallen combatants who chose death before dishonor. He dreamed of fighting alongside Caesar and Alexander the Great, Achilles and William the Conqueror, Washington and Sherman, and one day he too would order his charges to fight on some of the same battlefields his heroes fought on in centuries past.

Later, as a young man he walked the battlefields of the Civil War and envisioned how the Union and Confederate commanders maneuvered their forces. As a junior officer in the Great War, he would stand on hillsides, look out at the vast expanses, and imagine the invincible Roman Legions and the brutality of Attila and the Huns rampaging over the horizon, terrorizing all who dared to challenge them. He could feel the thunder of the Charge of the Light Brigade and the prestigious Polish cavalry (before they were cut down by the Nazi blitzkrieg during the fall of 1939).

He explored the fortresses and ramparts of North Africa and walked among the ruins of Sicily, conquered and conquered again by so many, and he said without hesitation, "I was there."

As a youngster, George S. Patton, Jr. (1885-1945), listened to tales of daring and yearned to someday be a great army commander. The cadet excelled in his studies at Virginia Military Institute,, knowing he was destined for greatness. (U.S. Military Academy)

He said it so often in so many places, and could recall in such detail how the battles had unfolded decades before, that many others thought just maybe he had been there. In a past life? Maybe. As a boy with a wild imagination and a voracious appetite to learn? Probably. As a student of war? Definitely.

More importantly, going into every engagement, General Patton, the leader of warriors, studied his opponent for tendencies, strengths, and weaknesses. He analyzed previous battles waged on the same terrain, even those many centuries ago, finding the keys to victory and the factors that led to defeat. This allowed him to develop contingency plans to counter any moves his enemy might try to turn the offensive to their advantage.

He studied changes in war fighting, such as the massed formations of the American Revolution and the Civil War, squaring off at fifty yards and decimating the enemy ranks. He had survived the trench warfare of World War I and despised it, and he read with fascination about this new "lightning warfare" developed by the Germans that utilized the combined forces of infantry, armor, artillery, and aviation to overwhelm an opponent.

By the end of World War II, Patton was credited with using blitzkrieg tactics even better than the Germans had. In fact, the German High Command feared Patton more than any other Allied leader because he was the most daring and the most successful.

Patton understood that, despite the advancements in weaponry—from the catapult to the howitzer, from the ball and musket to the machinegun—ultimately, wars were fought by warriors. He also knew that those armies that trained to be expedient and brutal, disciplined and ruthless would be victorious over any opponent that did not also have the supreme trait: a warrior's soul. Patton demanded that unforgiving warrior's soul from himself and every soldier in his command. While others served proudly with the Big Red

One, the Second Armored, the Screaming Eagles, the Tenth Mountain, or any of the many battle-tested units of the U.S. Army, those soldiers who stood the tallest would simply state years later, "I served with Patton." That's all they needed to say, and everyone understood.

Here then is a glimpse into the psyche and the recollections and the soul of the ultimate warrior . . . the incomparable George S. Patton, American World War II soldier par excellence.

"My poetry, my rhymes, were written by a man who, having seen something of war, is more impressed with the manly virtues it engenders than with the necessary and much exaggerated horrors attendant upon it. They are offered to the public in the hope that they may help to counteract the melancholy viewpoint of many of our poets who write of the great wars. We should not dwell on sorrow that these slain in battle have died, but rather be thankful that they have lived."
~ *Patton on his writings.*

THE
MAXIMS
OF
GENERAL
PATTON

As commander of the Second Armored Division, Maj. Gen. George Patton drilled his soldiers, preparing them for a war already escalating in Europe. During the Louisiana Maneuvers in 1941, he oversaw a company of combat engineers as they assembled a pontoon bridge. (Patton Museum)

Chapter 1

On Training and Technology

George Patton was a taskmaster, pushing his men to exhaustion day after day in simulated combat exercises, long before they ever felt the sting of battle. He knew that working together as a cohesive unit during war games in the States would lead to fewer casualties on the killing fields somewhere overseas. He preached "more sweat, less blood."

Some couldn't cut it, and many cursed his name, but he knew how important it was to sharpen the spear to a razor's edge. Every soldier needed to know his role as part of a formidable fighting force. That force had yet to experience the brutal ugliness of combat, but Patton was confident that, once thrown into the fire, it would quickly become an unstoppable blaze of American might.

By studying advances in weaponry and war fighting, by absorbing the writings of other combat tacticians such as Sun Tzu and Clausewitz—whose ideas of warfare clashed with his own views—Patton envisioned a fast-moving strike capability, as yet untested in combat . . . that is until July of 1936, when Nazi Germany sent the combined air and ground forces of the Condor Legion to Spain, fighting alongside the Nationalists in that country's civil war. The Nazis had unleashed their own form of this lightning warfare, known as the blitzkrieg.

Reading news reports of this devastating and formidable combined arms force, Patton knew this would be the future of warfare, and he would be America's main proponent, despite overwhelming criticism from his army contemporaries.

———

"The purposes of discipline and training are:
"1. To ensure obedience and orderly movement.
"2. To produce synthetic courage.
"3. To provide methods of combat.
"4. To prevent or delay the breakdown of the first three due to the excitement of battle.
"The Americans as a race are the greatest mechanic in the world. America as a nation has the greatest ability for mass production of machines. It therefore behooves us to devise methods of war which exploit our inherent superiority. We must fight the war by machines on the ground and in the air to the maximum of our ability." ~ *Journal entry*.

———

"Battle is an orgy of disorder. No level lawn nor marker flags exist to aid us in strutting ourselves in vain display, but rather groups of weary, wandering men seeking gropingly for means to kill their foes. The sudden change from accustomed order to utter disorder, to chaos, but emphasizes the folly of schooling to precision and obedience where only fierceness and habituated disorder are useful."

———

"When man first began fighting man, he unquestionably used his teeth, toenails and fingernails. Then one day a very terrified or else very inventive genius picked up a rock and bashed a man in the head while he was gnawing at his vitals. The news of this unheard-of weapon unquestionably shocked Neolithic Society, but they became accustomed to it. Thousands of years later, another genius picked up the splintered rib of a Mastodon and using it as a dagger, thrust it into the gentleman with a rock in his hand. Again, pre-historic society was shocked and said, 'There will surely be no more wars. Did you hear about the Mastodon bone?' When the shield, slingshot, javelin and the sword and armor were successively invented, each in its turn was heralded by the proponents as a means of destroying the world or of stopping war."

―――

"Do not regard what you do only as 'preparation' for doing the same thing more fully or better at some later time. Nothing is ever done twice. There is no next time. This is of special application to war. There is but one time to win a battle or a campaign. It must be won the first time."

―――

"History is replete with accounts of military inventions, each heralded by its disciples as the 'Dernier Cri'—the 'Key' to victory."

―――

"It is the common experience of mankind that in moments of great excitement the conscious mental processes of the brain no longer operate. All actions are subconscious, the result of habits. Troops whose training and discipline depend on conscious thought become helpless crowds in battle. To send forth such men is murder. Hence, in creating an Army, we must strive at the production of soldiers, so trained that in the midst of battle they will still function."

―――

"If brevity is the soul of wit, then repetition is the heart of instruction."

―――

"Today, machines hold the place formally [formerly] occupied by the jawbone of an ass, elephant, armor, longbow, gunpowder, and submarine. They, too, shall pass."

"Certainly, the advent of the atomic bomb was not half as startling as the initial appearance of gunpowder. In my own lifetime, I can remember two inventions, or possibly three, which were supposed to stop war; namely the dynamite cruiser 'Vesuvius,' the submarine and the tank. Yet, wars go blithely on and will still go on when your great-grandchildren are very old men."

"When the great day of battle comes, remember your training, and remember, above all, that speed and vigor of attack are the sure roads to success and that you must succeed. To retreat is as cowardly as it is fatal." ~ *Journal entry after Operation Torch, the invasion of North Africa, November 3, 1942.*

"It is very easy for ignorant people to think that success in war may be gained by the use of some wonderful invention rather than by hard fighting and superior leadership."

As a cadet at Virginia Military Institute and West Point, George Patton analyzed battles and studied terrain maps and had seen how many of his contemporaries relied on book knowledge to make command decisions. But he knew that, quite often, the human factor had more of an impact on a battle's outcome than even the terrain or weather.

"Since the necessary limitations of map problems inhibit the student from considering the effects of hunger, emotion, personality, fatigue, leadership and many other imponderable yet vital factors, he first neglects and then forgets them."

———

"The initial appearance of each new weapon or military device has always marked the zenith of its tactical effect, though usually the nadir of its technical efficiency."

———

"Americans pride themselves on being He Men and they *are* He Men. Remember that the enemy is just as frightened as you are and probably more so. They are not supermen.

"All through your Army careers, you men have bitched about what you call 'chicken-s— drilling.' That, like everything else in this Army, has a definite purpose. That purpose is alertness. Alertness must be bred into every soldier.

"I don't give a f— for a man who's not always on his toes. You men are veterans or you wouldn't be here. You are ready for what's to come. A man must be alert at all times if he expects to stay alive.

"If you're not alert, sometime, a German son-of-an-a–hole-bitch is going to sneak up behind you and beat you to death with a sockful of s—!"

With the conclusion of the European campaign, General Patton was decked out with sashes and medals, including numerous foreign awards, in June 1945. (Patton Museum)

Chapter 2

On Pride, Discipline, and Confidence

George Patton bled red, white and blue . . . the ultimate soldier and American patriot. He understood the sacrifices of fighting for Old Glory and the pride of wearing "colored strips of ribbon" on the chest.

Some might say he went a little overboard with the pomp and circumstance of the profession of war fighting, with the shiny pistols, the gleaming stars on his shoulders, and the pretty colored strips of ribbon plastered to his chest in neat rows, all gift-wrapped with sashes and lanyards. But Patton wanted every soldier in his command to take pride in his unit and his own accomplishments.

Patton demanded unit cohesion and expected every combatant to pull his share of the load, to do his part to achieve the mission. He expected nothing less than everyone's best.

———

"A young soldier, upon being asked by Napoleon what he desired in recompense for an heroic act said, 'Sire, the Legion of Honor,' to which Napoleon replied, 'My boy, you are over young for such an honor.' The soldier again said, 'Sire, in your service, we do not grow old.'

"This story is as true as it is tragic. Our men do not grow old. We must exploit their abilities and satisfy their longings to the utmost during the brief span of their existence. Surely, an inch of satin for a machinegun nest put out of action is a bargain not to be lightly passed up."

———

"If a man has done his best, what else is there? I consider that I have always done my best. My conscience is clear."

———

"This 'Blood and Guts' stuff is quite distasteful to me. I am a very severe disciplinarian because I know that without discipline it is impossible to win battles and that without discipline to send men into battle is to commit murder."

———

"You are not beaten until you admit it."

———

"The greatest privilege of citizenship is to be able to freely bear arms under one's country's flag."

———

"No sane man is not afraid in battle, but discipline produces in him a form of vicarious courage which, with his manhood, makes for victory. Self-respect grows directly from discipline. The Army saying, 'Whoever saw a dirty soldier with a medal?' is largely true. Pride, in turn, stems from self-respect and from the knowledge that the soldier is an American." ~ *Journal entry.*

———

"The soldier is the army. No army is better than the soldiers in it. To be a good soldier, a man must have discipline, self confidence, self respect, pride in his unit and in his country. He must have a high sense of duty and obligation to his comrades and to his superiors." ~ *Journal entry.*

———

"Remember this: no set piece of tactics is of any merit in itself unless it is executed by heroic and disciplined troops who have self confidence and who have leaders who take care of them."

———

"In my opinion, we will only win this war through blood, sacrifice, and courage. In order to get willing fighters, we must develop the highest possible 'Esprit de Corps.' Therefore, the removal of distinctive badges and insignia from the uniform is highly detrimental. To die willingly, as many of us must, we must have tremendous pride not only in our nation and in ourselves, but also in the unit to which we belong."

———

"To me, it is a never ending marvel what our soldiers can do."

———

"Discipline must be a habit so ingrained that it is stronger than the excitement of battle or the fear of death."

———

"Discipline, which is but mutual trust and confidence, is the key to all success in peace or war."

———

"The important thing in any organization is the creation of a soul, which is based on pride, in the unit."

———

"The flag is to the patriot what the cross is to the Christian."

———

"The most vital quality which a soldier can possess is self confidence; utter, complete and bumptious. You can have doubts about your good looks, about your intelligence, or about your self control, but to win in war, you must have no doubt about your ability as a soldier."

Chapter 3

Patton's Fury

George Patton was a lit fuse, always on the verge of exploding at any moment.

He studied battle tactics and the bold decisions and critical mistakes commanders made under fire. Caesar, Hannibal, Sherman, Alexander the Great . . . he examined them all, absorbing their philosophies and adapting them to mesh with his own. By studying the great military leaders and assessing his own successes, he understood there was a fine line between victory and defeat. It was sometimes as simple as a commander hesitating for a few hours or sending his forces exactly where the enemy was positioned to devastate them.

He pushed his forces hard, believing that sweat in war games stateside would minimize the amount of blood spilled once they got thrown into battle, and he lashed out at anyone not performing at his best. This applied to everyone—his subordinate commanders most of all. And when they did not measure up to his expectations, he exploded with venom and fury and did not hesitate to replace them. Indecision, incompetence, and cowardice could set him off quicker than anything else. He knew that each of those could lead to needless casualties on the battlefield.

Patton hated delays, constantly preaching the importance of rapid advance. During the invasion of North Africa, America's first real combat action against Nazi Germany, Major General Patton was itching to get ashore with his troops, while his landing craft was left to dangle alongside the cruiser Augusta, which was engaged in battle. The longer he had to wait, the angrier he got. (National Archives)

"From time to time there will be some complaints that we are pushing our people too hard. I don't give a good G–damn about such complaints. I believe in the old and sound rule that an ounce of sweat will save a gallon of blood.

"The harder *we* push, the more Germans we will kill. The more Germans we kill, the fewer of our men will be killed. Pushing means fewer casualties. I want you all to remember that." ~ *Patton at a Third Army staff conference, July 31, 1944.*

"Never stop being ambitious. You have but one life; live it to the fullest of glory and be willing to pay any price."

"You must never halt because some other unit is stuck. If you push on, you will relieve the pressure on the adjacent unit and it will accompany you."

"We must remember that victories are not gained solely by selfless devotion. To conquer, we must destroy our enemies. We must not only die gallantly, we must kill devastatingly. The faster and more effectively we kill, the longer we will live to enjoy the priceless fame of conquerors."

"Cowardice is a disease and it must be checked."

"I am a soldier, I fight where I am told, and I win where I fight."

"The fixed determination to acquire the warrior soul, and

having acquired it, to conquer or perish with honor, is the secret of success in war."

"My men don't surrender. I don't want to hear of any soldier under my command being captured unless he has been hit. Even if you are hit, you can still fight back. That's not just bulls— either. The kind of man that I want in my command is just like the lieutenant in Libya, who, with a Luger against his chest, jerked off his helmet, swept the gun aside with one hand and busted the hell out of the Kraut with his helmet. Then he jumped on the gun and went out and killed another German before they knew what the hell was coming off. And, all of that time, this man had a bullet through a lung. There was a real man!"

"War is a bloody, killing business. You've got to spill their blood, or they will spill yours. Rip them up the belly. Shoot them in the guts." ~ *Patton to the Second Armored Division at Fort Benning, 1941.*

"Of course, our men are willing to die, but that is not enough. We must be eager to kill, to inflict on the enemy, the hated enemy, all possible wounds, death and destruction.

"If we die killing, well and good. But, if we fight hard enough, viciously enough, we will kill and live to kill again. We will live to return to our families as conquering heroes."

"Many of you have in your veins German and Italian blood. But remember that these ancestors of yours so loved freedom that they gave up home and country to cross the ocean in search of liberty. The ancestors of the people we shall kill lacked the courage to make such a sacrifice and remained slaves." ~ *From Patton's Order of the Day as his Seventh Army assaulted Sicily, July 1943.*

———

"I also re-read the 'Norman Conquest' by Freeman, paying particular attention to the roads used by William the Conqueror during his operations in Normandy and Brittany. The roads used in those days had to be on ground which was always practical." ~ *Journal entry, August 1 to September 24, 1944.*

———

"We have got by due to persistence and on the ability to make plans fit circumstances. The other armies try to make circumstances fit plans."

———

"When shells are hitting all around you and you wipe the dirt off your face and realize that instead of dirt it's the blood and guts of what once was your best friend beside you, you'll know what to do!"

———

"When a man is lying in a shell hole, if he just stays there all day, a German will get to him eventually. The hell with that idea. The hell with taking it. My men don't dig foxholes. I don't want them to. Foxholes only slow up an offensive. Keep moving. And don't give the enemy time to dig one either.

"We'll win this war, but we'll win it only by fighting and by showing the Germans that we've got more guts than they have; or ever will have. We're not going to just shoot the sons-of-bitches, we're going to rip out their living Godd— guts and use them to grease the treads of our tanks. We're going to murder those lousy Hun c–ksuckers by the bushel-f—ing-basket."

———

"My policy of continuous attack is correct. The farther we press, the more stuff we find abandoned that should not be abandoned. The Italians are fighting very well in the face of defeat. They must crack soon."

———

"It lurks invisible in that vitalizing spark, intangible, yet as evident as the lightning: the 'Warrior Soul.'"

———

"War is conflict. Fighting is an elemental exposition of the age old effort to survive. It is the cold glitter of the attacker's eye that breaks the line, not the point of the bayonet."

———

"Now if you are going to win any battle you have to do one thing. You have to make the mind run the body. Never let the body tell the mind what to do. The body will always give up. It is always tired morning, noon, and night. But the body is never tired if the mind is not tired. When you were younger the mind could make you dance all night, and the body was never tired. . . . You've always got to make the mind take over and keep going."

———

"Unless you do your best, the day will come when, tired and hungry, you will halt just short of the goal you were ordered to reach and by halting, you will make useless the efforts and deaths of thousands."

Chapter 4

On Teamwork and Sports

Teamwork on the battlefield meant utilizing every element available—the firepower of aviation and artillery in support of the fast-moving armor and infantry as they engaged the enemy; a well-oiled supply route to move provisions to the front; a medical pipeline to evacuate casualties to aid stations and field hospitals as quickly as possible; and a communications network to maintain contact up and down the line, to respond immediately to enemy movement on the battlefield, and then counterpunch with devastating force. No commander did this better than General Patton. No commander trusted in his team more, confident they would succeed in battle while other Allied commanders marveled at their achievements and audacity.

Patton simply knew what his units were made of, and he understood that every soldier had a job to do and was a vital cog in the machinery of the U.S. Army. He expected everyone to do their jobs and know the responsibilities of the others in their unit, should they fall in combat. This ensured that every member of the team remained connected to the next in an unbreakable, impenetrable chain. Patton demanded nothing less, and his soldiers never failed him.

"All of the real heroes are not storybook combat fighters.

George Patton was enough of an athlete to compete in the Pentathlon at the Stockholm Olympics. He certainly understood the importance of teamwork within an army unit and wanted everyone cross-trained and prepared for any mission. Here he is talking to his troops soon after they made it to Sicily. (Patton Museum)

Every single man in this Army plays a vital role. Don't ever let up. Don't ever think that your job is unimportant. Every man has a job to do and he must do it. Every man is a vital link in the great chain. What if every truck driver suddenly decided that he didn't like the whine of those shells overhead, turned yellow and jumped headlong into a ditch? The cowardly bastard could say, 'Hell, they won't miss me, just one man in thousands.'

"But, what if every man thought that way? Where in the hell would we be now? What would our country, our loved ones, our homes, even the world, be like? No, Godd— it, Americans don't think like that.

"Every man does his job. Every man serves the whole. Every department, every unit, is important in the vast scheme of this war.

"The ordnance men are needed to supply the guns and machinery of war to keep us rolling. The Quartermaster is needed to bring up food and clothes because where we are going there isn't a hell of a lot to steal. Every last man on K.P. has a job to do, even the one who heats our water to keep us from getting the 'G.I. S—s.'" ~ *Patton to various units of the Third Army in England, March to May 1944.*

———

"A tank fight is just like a barroom fight—the fellow who gets the hit wins. Our men, especially in the 4th Armored, are magnificent shots. The 4th, 2nd and 3rd Armored are old divisions and have plenty of practice. I used to train them to get on a target of 30 degrees off target in three seconds. They did not do it, but they got awfully fast. . . .

"The whole thing in tank fighting is to train crews not as individuals but as crews." ~ *Patton at a news conference, September 23, 1944.*

———

"I believe that in war, the good of the individual must be subordinated to the good of the Army."

———

"The wrestling adage, 'There is a block for every hold' is equally applicable to war. Each new weapon demands a new block and it is mightily potent until that block is devised."

———

"When, at the beginning of the football season the quarterback barks his numbers at the crouching players, he excites an innate opposition; the feeling of 'why in the hell should I do what he says?' Yet until that feeling is banished by habit, the team is dead on its feet.

"The soldier at attention and saluting, is putting himself in the same frame of mind as the player; alert, on his toes, receptive.

"In battle, the officers are the quarterbacks, the men are the disciplined team on their toes, with that lightning response to orders which means victory and the lack of which means death and defeat."

———

"War is just like boxing. When you get your opponent on the ropes you must keep punching the hell out of him and not let him recover."

———

"The spirit of the men in the Evacuation Hospitals was improving and the incidence of 'battle fatigue' and of 'self inflicted wounds' had dropped materially. Soldiers like to play on a winning team."

———

"Battle is not a terrifying ordeal to be endured. It is a magnificent experience wherein all of the elements that have made man superior to the beasts are present. Courage, self sacrifice, loyalty, help to others and devotion to duty.

"As you go in, you will perhaps be a little short of breath, and your knees may tremble. This breathlessness, this tremor, they are not fear. It is simply the excitement which every athlete feels just before the whistle blows.

"No, you will not fear, for you will be borne up and exalted by the proud instinct of our conquering race. You will be inspired by magnificent hate."

"There are four hundred neatly marked graves somewhere in Sicily, all because one man went to sleep on the job. But they are German graves, because we caught the bastard asleep before they did.

"An Army is a team. It lives, sleeps, eats and fights as a team. This individual heroic stuff is pure horse s—. The bilious bastards who write that kind of stuff for the *Saturday Evening Post* don't know any more about real fighting under fire than they know about f—ing!" ~ *Patton to various units of the Third Army in England, March to May 1944.*

"Lack of discipline at play means the loss of the game. Lack of discipline in war means death or defeat, which is worse than death. The prize of a game is nothing. The prize of war is the greatest of all prizes . . . Freedom."

"When you, here, every one of you, were kids, you all admired the champion marble player, the fastest runner, the toughest boxer, the big league ball players and the All-American football players.

"Americans love a winner. Americans will not tolerate a loser. Americans despise cowards. Americans play to win all of the time. I wouldn't give a hoot in hell for a man who lost and laughed. That's why Americans have never lost nor will ever lose a war; for the very idea of losing is hateful to an American." ~ *Patton to various units of the Third Army in England, March to May 1944.*

"To achieve harmony in battle, each weapon must support the other. Team play wins. You 'musicians' of Mars must not wait for the band leader to signal to you. You must, each of your own volition, see to it that you come into this concert at the proper time and at the proper place."

"Wars may be fought with weapons, but they are won by men. It is the spirit of the men who follow and the man who leads that gains the victory."

"You should have seen those trucks on the road to Tunisia. Those drivers were magnificent. All day and all night they rolled over those son-of-a-bitching roads, never stopping, never faltering from their course, with shells bursting all around them all of the time. We got through on good old American guts.

"Many of those men drove for over forty consecutive hours. These men weren't combat men, but they were soldiers with a job to do. They did it and in one hell of a way they did it. They were part of a team.

"Without team effort, without them, the fight would have been lost. All of the links in the chain pulled together and the chain became unbreakable."

Chapter 5

Patton's Humor

George Patton frequently got into trouble for things he said, but that did not deter him from further utterances. Some were spontaneous, others calculated, but the result was often hilarious. While his superiors cringed every time they learned of another Patton faux pas, they also knew he meant what he said and said what he meant. Sometimes, just maybe he said exactly what they were thinking but were a little too diplomatic to say it. Such was the case during the fighting in Europe, when Russia was a key partner and defeated the Nazis on the Eastern Front after brutal and costly months of sustained fighting. Patton hated the Russians and did not hide his feelings. He believed that once Hitler was defeated, Stalin would be America's next enemy, a belief borne out years later during the Cold War.

As cold and callous as Patton appeared, especially to members of the press corps, he did have a wicked sense of humor, though not many appreciated his acid tongue.

"I don't want to get any messages saying, 'I am holding my position.' We are not holding a Godd— thing. Let the Germans do that. We are advancing constantly and we are not

Army artist Bill Mauldin was very popular with other American soldiers for his scruffy, unshaven characters Willie and Joe. Patton hated the portrayal and summoned Mauldin for a thorough tongue-lashing. After the meeting, Mauldin joked that Patton and his bull terrier, Willie, presented the meanest pairs of eyes he had ever encountered! Here with his staff, Lieutenant General Patton waits impatiently for the arrival of General Eisenhower. Despite Patton's no-nonsense persona, he actually had a sense of humor, often brutal and sometimes risqué. (U.S. Army)

interested in holding onto anything, except the enemy's balls. We are going to twist his balls and kick the living s— out of him all of the time.

"Our basic plan of operation is to advance and to keep on advancing regardless of whether we have to go over, under, or through the enemy. We are going to go through him like crap through a goose; like s— through a tin horn!"

———

"The only thing to do when a son of a bitch looks cross-eyed at you is to beat the hell out of him right then and there."

———

"Sure, we want to go home. We want this war over with. The quickest way to get it over with is to go get the bastards who started it.

"The quicker they are whipped, the quicker we can go home. The shortest way home is through Berlin and Tokyo. And when we get to Berlin, I am personally going to shoot that paper hanging son-of-a-bitch Hitler. Just like I'd shoot a snake!"

———

"I saw a lot of dead Germans yesterday frozen in funny attitudes. I got some good pictures, but did not have my color camera, which was a pity, as they were a pale claret color."

———

"We are going to kill German bastards. I would prefer to skin them alive, but gentlemen, I fear some of our people at home would accuse me of being too rough."

———

"We want to get the hell over there. The quicker we clean up this Godd— mess, the quicker we can take a little jaunt against the purple pissing Japs and clean out their nest too. Before the Godd— Marines get all of the credit."

There is a fine line between combat and religion. Men trained as warriors want nothing more than peace, but sometimes it requires brutality to rid the world of dictators such as Adolf Hitler.

Going into battle, soldiers on both sides pray to the same God, but He rarely chooses sides. George Patton noted the dilemma soon after his forces made it to France:

"The first Sunday I spent in Normandy was quite impressive. I went to a Catholic Field Mass where all of us were armed.

"As we knelt in the mud in the slight drizzle, we could distinctly hear the roar of the guns, and the whole sky was filled with airplanes on their missions of destruction . . . quite at variance with the teachings of the religion we were practicing."

George Patton could put the fear of God into any man, but he also believed that sometimes maybe a little divine intervention wouldn't hurt. After enduring continuous rain across northern Europe in early December of 1944, General Patton was desperate for a miracle. By midmonth, he summoned Col. T. H. O'Neill, the Third Army chaplain, and requested that he write a prayer asking the Lord to halt the rain. "May I say, General, that it usually isn't a customary thing among men of my profession to pray for clear weather to kill fellow men," the chaplain explained, to no avail. Patton knew what he wanted, and that was a prayer to stop the damn rain so he could get on with the messy business of killing Krauts!

The chaplain fought with his inner demons but in the end wrote Patton's "Prayer to Halt the Rain," which would be printed on the back of a Christmas greeting and distributed to all of the troops in his command on December 23.

While not actually written by Patton, it was attributed to

him. It was also debated as to whether or not he really believed in the power of the Almighty. But on Christmas Eve, the rains stopped, the storm clouds departed, and clear skies prevailed for six days straight. Patton ordered his troops to resume the offensive, to get back to the business of killing Krauts!

"Christmas dawned clear and cold; lovely weather for killing Germans, although the thought seemed somewhat at variance with the spirit of the day," Patton wrote in his journal.

The Prayer to Halt the Rain . . . (and resume the killing!)

Almighty and most merciful Father, we humbly beseech Thee,
or Thy great goodness, to restrain these immoderate rains
with which we have had to contend.

Grant us fair weather for Battle.
Graciously hearken to us as soldiers who call upon Thee that,
armed with Thy power, we may advance from victory to victory,
and crush the oppression and wickedness of our enemies,
and establish Thy justice among men and nations. Amen.

While other Allied commanders, such as Britain's Bernard Montgomery, leaned toward a slow and methodical approach to warfare, George Patton wanted to throw lightning bolts, get the Nazi forces on the run, and keep on pushing them all the way back to Berlin. It was inconceivable to him that a lack of fuel—his tanks needed 400,000 gallons every day—could stall the advance across France, but he was ordered to stand down and wait for the British to catch up. Patton couldn't resist taking a verbal shot at Monty:

"Take this five gallon gasoline can to Montgomery with this message: 'Although I am sadly short of gasoline myself, I know of your admiration for our equipment and supplies and I can spare you this five gallons. It will be more than enough to take you as far as you probably will advance in the next two days.'"

Weeks later, as Allied forces raced across France and approached the Rhine River, it was reported through British channels that Montgomery's forces were first to cross into Germany, even though Patton's own forces had bounced the Rhine two days earlier! Patton loved rubbing Monty's nose in it.

"The 21st Army Group was supposed to cross the Rhine River on 24th March, 1945 and in order to be ready for this 'earthshaking' event, Mr. Churchill wrote a speech congratulating Field Marshal Montgomery on the 'first' assault crossing over the Rhine River in modern history. This speech was recorded and through some error on the part of the British Broadcasting Corporation, was broadcast. In spite of the fact that the [American] Third Army had been across the Rhine River for some *thirty-six hours.* "

Due to the attritions of war, replacements were sent forward to ensure that American units maintained their fighting strength. But typically these untested combatants quickly became casualties.

General Patton recognized this and called on his battle-hardened veterans to bond with these rookies, for the good of the unit: "War develops a soul in a fighting unit, and where there may not be many of the old men left, it takes very little yeast to leaven a lump of dough. I suppose I might be funny and say it takes very few veterans to leaven a division of doughboys."

The quicker these new combatants acquired the "warrior soul" Patton demanded, the more likely they were to survive to later tell about their experiences in World War II.

Prior to the D-Day invasion, Patton was reassigned to England to command a fictitious invasion force. The plan was to fool the Germans into redeploying their units away from Normandy. Patton travelled across southern England during the first half of 1944, making numerous speeches to his troops, knowing enemy spies would promptly report his whereabouts and whatever he might say. At one appearance, he declared:

"Don't forget, you men don't know that I'm here. No mention of that fact is to be made in any letters. The world is not supposed to know what the hell happened to me. I'm not supposed to be commanding this Army. I'm not even supposed to be here in England. Let the first bastards to find out be the Godd— Germans.

"Someday I want to see them raise up on their piss-soaked hind legs and howl, 'Jesus Christ, it's the Godd— Third Army again and that son-of-a-f—ing-bitch Patton.'"

"The grave of that national hero, 'Abandoned Rear,' was still maintained by the [French] natives. It originated in this manner: In 1917, the mayor, who lived in the 'new house' at Bourg, bearing the date 1760, came to me, weeping copiously, to say that we had failed to tell him of the death of one of my soldiers.

"Being unaware of this sad fact and not liking to admit it to a stranger, I stalled until I found out that no one was dead. However, he insisted that we visit the 'grave,' so we went together and found a newly closed latrine pit with the earth properly banked and a stick at one end to which was affixed crosswise a sign saying, 'Abandoned Rear.' This the French had taken for a cross. I never told them the truth."

Even when he was trying to pay a compliment, George Patton had a way of saying things that got him in hot water:

"After nearly two years of being accustomed to the inarticulate shapes of the Arab women, the over-stuffed profiles of the Italians, and to the boyish figures of the British women, the obtrusive and meticulously displayed figures of the Norman and Brittan women is quite striking. In a way they remind me of a British engine with two bumpers in front and powerful driving wheels behind."

———

George Patton, serious scholar of war craft, also liked to try his hand at poetry, such as taking a sarcastic poke at befuddled bureaucrats and simpleton staff weenies he encountered when he wasn't doing more important things, such as conquering foreign lands:

REFERENCE: BandB3c-24614, FILE: INV. FORM A62B-M.Q.

As Head of the Division of Provision for Revision
    Was a man of prompt decision: Morton Quirk.
Ph.D. in Calisthenics, P.D.Q. in Pathogenics.
    He has just the proper background for the work.

From the pastoral aroma of Aloma, Oklahoma
    With a pittance of a salary in hand,
His acceptance had been whetted, even aided and abetted
    By emolument that netted some five grand.

So, with energy ecstatic, this fanatic left his attic
    and hastened on to Washington, D.C.
Where with verve and vim and vigor, he went hunting for the N—
    In the woodpile of the W.P.B.

After months of patient process Morton's [peculiar] proboscis
    Had unearthed a reprehensible hiatus
In reply by Blair and Blair to his thirteenth questionnaire
    In connection with their inventory status.

They had written—"Your directive when effective was defective
    "In its ultimate objective and what's more

"Neolithic hieroglyphic is, to us, much more specific
    "than the drivel you keep dumping at our door."

This sacrilege discovered, Morton fainted, but recovered
    Sufficiently to write, "We are convinced
"that sabotage is camouflaged behind perverted persiflage.
    "Expect me on the 22nd inst."

But first he sent a checker, then he sent a checker's checker
    Still nothing was disclosed as being wrong.
So a checker's checker's checker came to check the checker's
       checker
    and the process was laborious and long.

Then followed a procession of the follow-up profession
    Through the records of the firm of Blair and Blair.
From the breakfast until supper some new super-follow-upper
    Tore his fair because of Morton's questionnaire.

The file is closed, completed, though our Hero, undefeated
    Carries on in some department as before.
And vict'ry is in sight of, not because of, but in spite of
    Doctor Morton's mighty efforts in the war.

"We have the finest food, the finest equipment, the best spirit and the best men in the world. Why, by God, I actually pity those poor sons-of-bitches we're going up against. By God, I do."

"One of the bravest men that I ever saw was a fellow on top of a telegraph pole in the midst of a furious firefight in Tunisia. I stopped and asked what the hell he was doing up there at a time like that. He answered, 'Fixing the wire, Sir.' I asked, 'Isn't that a little unhealthy right about now?' He answered, 'Yes Sir, but the Godd--- wire has to be fixed.' I asked, 'Don't those planes strafing the road bother you?'

And he answered, 'No, Sir, but you sure as hell do!'

"Now, there was a real man. A real soldier. There was a man who devoted all he had to his duty, no matter how seemingly insignificant his duty might appear at the time, no matter how great the odds."

One of the most memorable Patton quotes, humorous and succinct, sums up exactly how he felt about war:

"No bastard ever won a war by dying for his country. He won it by making the other poor dumb bastard die for his country."

Chapter 6

On Soldiering Skills

He was the brash gunslinger, the World War I combatant wounded in battle and hardened by the prolonged miseries of trench warfare. George Patton vowed to never get caught up in another defensive engagement in the next conflict, most likely in Europe, most likely in the very near future. He trained his troops beyond the breaking point, indifferent to their feelings, but he knew that their lives might depend on honing their soldiering skills.

In 1939 and '40, large-scale war games were held in Louisiana to test and coordinate the combined forces of the army, with mixed results. When mounted cavalry forces came up against Patton's armored forces, it was an overwhelming victory for the tankers. (The Nazi blitzkrieg had similar results when they invaded Poland and decimated its highly respected mounted cavalry. The old way of fighting wars had little chance against this new unconventional juggernaut unleashed by the Nazis.)

Fully believing that only the most disciplined army would be victorious on the battlefield, Patton honed his "bayonet psychology" to a razor-sharp edge, so that his enemies feared an encounter with him.

Never one to shun the spotlight, Major General Patton, commander of the Second Armored Division, wanted a distinctive uniform to separate his armor crewmen from other army soldiers. He came up with a jumpsuit, and soon everyone called him the Green Hornet! As the U.S. Army's strongest advocate for armored warfare, Patton foresaw the evolution of ground combat, with the tank leading the charge. (Patton Museum)

"War means fighting and fighting means killing."

———

"War is not a contest with gloves. It is resorted to only when laws, which are rules, have failed."

———

With his own son at West Point, Patton gave him some fatherly advice on June 6, 1944:

"What you must know is how man reacts. Weapons change, but man who uses them changes not at all. To win battles you do not beat weapons . . . you beat the soul of the enemy."

That "soul" was the individual soldier, and Patton truly believed that the American G.I. was better than any combatant his son would face in battle.

———

"When any group of soldiers is under small arms fire, it is evident that the enemy can see them; therefore, men should be able to see the enemy but seldom are. When this situation arises, they must fire at the portions of the hostile terrain which probably conceal enemy small arms weapons.

"I know for a fact that such procedure invariably produces an effect and generally stops hostile fire. Always remember that it is much better to waste ammunition than lives. It takes at least eighteen years to produce a soldier and only a few months to produce ammunition."

———

"I'm proud to fight here beside you. Now let's cut the guts out of those Krauts and get the Hell to Berlin."

———

"There can never be too many projectiles in a battle. Whether they are thrown by cannon, rockets, or recoilless devices is immaterial. The purpose of all these instruments is identical . . . namely, to deluge the enemy with fire." ~ *Journal entry*.

———

"The true objective of armor is enemy infantry and artillery; and above all else, his supply installations and command centers."

———

"Each form of specialist, like the aviators, the artillery men, or the tanks, talk as if theirs was the only useful weapon and that if there were enough of them used, the war would soon end.

"As a matter of fact, it is the doughboy, in the final analysis, who does the trick."

———

General Patton pushed his soldiers hard and required them to develop a "warrior soul," and if they died in battle, then they died as heroes. If they were wounded in battle, Patton expected them to have the very best of care. He had little tolerance for cowards, those who feigned psychological trauma or accidentally on purpose shot themselves in the foot. He would have strung them up if it was his choice, or at least mustered them out of his unit. In two instances, while visiting field hospitals, Patton verbally lashed out and slapped soldiers he felt were less than heroic. It was his way of "motivating" them, but others did not agree with his methods.

Once the news got out, he was ordered to apologize to every man in his command, and then he was reassigned back to England, where he was forced to wait indefinitely for his next assignment. He just hoped it wouldn't take too long to get back in the fight to conquer Nazi Germany.

———

"Our men are really grim fighters. I would hate to be the enemy."

―――

"Go until the last shot is fired and the last drop of gasoline is gone. Then go forward on foot."

―――

As an avid student of warfare and its tactics, General Patton sought to achieve the advantage in every skirmish while minimizing his troops' exposure to danger. But every once in a while, there was an exception that proved that his theories could possibly be trumped by the presence of the Almighty:

"An amusing incident occurred on this trip. I have always insisted that anti-tank guns be placed where they can see without being seen. I came to a crucifix in the middle of a three-way road junction and sitting exactly under the crucifix was an anti-tank gun completely unconcealed.

"I gave the NCO in charge the devil for not having carried out my instructions. When I got through he said, 'Yes sir, but yesterday we got two tanks from this position.'

"So I had to apologize. Perhaps the sanctity of the location saved the gun?" ~ *Journal entry, August 1 to September 24, 1944.*

―――

"Americans do not surrender."

―――

"Americans love to fight. All real Americans love the sting of battle."

Many of his peers felt that George Patton was quick to pull the trigger and throw his soldiers into a campaign without any forethought. What they may not have known was that, prior to every engagement, Patton studied previous campaigns on the same battlegrounds, even going back centuries to analyze how terrain and weather impacted the outcome, what went wrong, and why. He also studied the current enemy commanders, probing for weaknesses he could exploit on the battlefield. Once this knowledge was absorbed, he not only knew the best course of action but prepared for any contingencies that might arise. Here, during the battles on Sicily, Lieutenant General Patton talks with Brig. Gen. Theodore Roosevelt, Jr., in August 1943. (National Archives)

Chapter 7

The Art of War

George Patton started his military career as a cavalry officer and was adept at handling the horse and the saber. He played polo with fellow World War II commander Lucian Truscott in their early years. And he represented the United States at the 1912 Olympics in Stockholm, placing fifth in the modern Pentathlon. Then he remained overseas to refine his skills at the French Cavalry School.

After returning to the States, he was assigned to the army's Mounted Service School at Fort Riley in Kansas, where he was the school's first Master of the Sword. He also redesigned the cavalry saber, which became known as the Patton Saber.

With advancements in warfare, it became possible to obliterate the enemy from safe distances. But General Patton rightfully believed there would be instances when combatants faced each other in close quarters, and then the survivor would be the only one who knew how to thrust and parry . . . with a saber or bayonet.

———

"Few men are killed by the bayonet; many are scared by it. Bayonets should be fixed when the firefight starts."

"Gentlemen, it cannot be done without mental practice. Therefore, you must school yourselves to savagery. You must imagine how it will feel when your sword hilt crashes into the breastbone of your enemy. You must picture the wild exaltation of the mounted charge when the lips are drawn back into a snarl and the voice cracks with a passion. At one time, you must be both a wise man and a fool."

"The XX Corps had captured intact . . . the whole of the Imperial Spanish Riding Academy which had left Vienna on the approach of the Russians. This Academy had been running in Vienna since the time of Charles V of Spain.

"Originally the gyrations taught the horses were of military importance. That is, the Courbette, or half-rear, was for the purpose of letting the horse come down at the same time that the sword was swung, so as to give the latter more force; the Volte, or Demi-Volte, was for the purpose of avoiding attack; while the leap into the air, striking out fore and aft with the feet, was for the purpose of extricating the rider from too close contact with the enemy, and so on.

"With the passing years and changes in the art of war, the purpose of this form of equitation was forgotten and the movements were taught as of value in themselves. In other words, people began, as in many other arts, to glorify the means rather than the end which the means were supposed to produce. . . .

"It struck me as rather strange that, in the midst of a world at war, some twenty young and middle-aged men in great physical condition, together with about thirty grooms, had spent their entire time teaching a group of horses to wiggle their butts and raise their feet in consonance with certain signals from the heels and reins. Much as I like horses, this seemed to me wasted energy. On the other hand, it is probably wrong to permit any highly developed art, no matter how fatuous, to perish from the earth—and which arts are fatuous depends on the point of view.

"To me the high-schooling of horses is certainly more interesting than either painting or music." ~ *Journal entry, May 1945.*

———

"The fear of having their guts explored with cold steel in the hands of battle maddened men has won many a fight."

———

Armored behemoths were introduced to the battlefield during the Great War, and George Patton was the first American commander attracted to the potential of tank warfare. In 1917, he led the fledgling United States Tank Corps when it first tasted victory, at Cambrai in France. A year later, he was directing his armor units at the front near the Meuse-Argonne offensive when he was wounded in the leg.

At great personal peril, Patton would continue to lead his troops at the front in World War II. Though he was widely recognized as a brilliant tactician in armor strategy, Patton was constantly expanding his encyclopedic knowledge of battle tactics, looking for any advantage.

After an exchange between German and American tanks on Sicily, he visited the site, where the disabled and burned-out metal hulks remained. He walked among the wrecked giants and noted in his diary:

"The majority of tanks put out first had their tracks shot off. I believe that we cannot too strongly emphasize shooting low. The German track is not so good and a hit with almost anything will go through it."

Many shells that were aimed high just glanced off the armor

plating of the German tanks. But if the tracks are destroyed, the tank can't maneuver, and it becomes a sitting duck.

Instead of futilely trying to destroy a tank, it merely required crippling it. Then the crew in the disabled tank would be forced to open their hatches and expose themselves to small-arms fire. Patton quickly dispatched this vital information to his subordinate tank commanders and shared it with his counterparts.

Following the Battle of the Bulge, Patton analyzed damage from enemy bombardment in the Huertgen Forest:

"I drove . . . through the forest which we had attacked so heavily with artillery during the Bastogne operation. The effect of the use of proximity fuse on the forest was very remarkable. You could see the exact angle of impact of all the projectiles, which had burst about 30 feet above the highest treetops. After bursting, they cut the trees at an angle of about 40 degrees down near the ground.

"However, it seemed to me then . . . that, in heavy woods, the proximity fuse is not efficient, as the timber absorbs the fragments. For such woods the delayed action fuse, which bursts only on hitting heavy trees close to the ground, is preferable. One continues to learn about war by practicing war." ~ *Journal entry, February 12, 1945.*

"No one realizes the terrible value of the 'unforgiving minute' except me. Someway I will get on yet," Patton wrote in his journal in late August of 1944 during the march across France.

By March of 1945, Patton's Third Army had "bounced the Rhine," the final obstacle as Allied forces pushed into the Fatherland. He ordered them to get across as quickly as possible, knowing how perilous river crossings could be, with troops vulnerable to enemy gunners waiting on the other side.

As he was crossing over on a pontoon bridge, Patton stopped to spit in the Rhine. (Some accounts stated he took the opportunity to relieve himself.)

Then, as he got to the other side, he deliberately stumbled, reenacting what William the Conqueror and Scipio Africanus had done many years before, when they too tripped, grabbed a handful of soil, and claimed the conquered territories as their own.

"Throughout history, wars have been lost because of armies not crossing rivers." ~ *Journal entry, August 1 to September 24, 1944.*

In 1944, Patton wrote about an amusing sight that reminded him of World War I:

"We drove on to Bourg, my tank brigade headquarters in 1918. The first man I saw in the street was standing on the same manure pile whereon I am sure he had perched in 1918. I asked if he had been there during the last war, to which he replied, 'Oh yes, General Patton, and you were here then as a colonel.'"

"The psychology of the fighting man is a strange thing. Early, well before dawn, I watched men of an almost green division, who were soaking wet and cold, cross a swollen river in the face of steep hills which were packed with concrete gun emplacements, machine guns, mines, and barbed wire. They crossed without hesitation and they walked right through that concentration of fire. They never hesitated once.

"Later in the day, I came across another outfit which was stalled along an open road. Do you know what was holding them back? It was a length of yellow string which was tied across their path between trees. No one in the outfit dared to touch it. I guess that it is the unknown which a man faces that he is scared of."

"Put your heart and soul into being expert killers with your weapons."

"Civilization has affected us. We abhor personal encounter. Many a man will risk his life, with an easy mind, in a burning house who would recoil from having his nose punched. We have been taught restraint from our emotions, to look upon anger as low, until many of us have never experienced the God sent ecstasy of unbridled wrath.

"We have never felt our eyes screw up, our temples throb and have never had the red mist gather in our sight. But, we expect that a man shall, in an instant, in the twinkling of an eye, divest himself of all restraint, of all caution and hurl himself upon the enemy, a frenzied beast, lusting to probe his enemy's guts with three feet of steel or to shatter his brain with a bullet."

"The night attack was interesting, because they had to advance through a mine field. They chose to do it in the dark and, as a result, lost 35 men. Had they advanced in the daytime, they would probably have lost the same 35 men to mines and, in addition, several hundred men to machine gun and rifle fire." ~ *Journal entry, November 8 to December 8, 1944.*

"At midnight on the night of December 31st, 1944 all guns in the Third Army fired rapid fire for twenty minutes on the Germans as a New Year's greeting. When the firing ceased, our forward observers stated they could hear the Germans screaming in the woods." ~ *Journal entry, December 19, 1944, to January 28, 1945.*

Chapter 8

Early Poems

As literature, George Patton's poems fall far short of being masterpieces. But as insights into this complex man, these early poems reveal a leader who cared more for his fellow soldiers than maybe he ever allowed anyone to see.

Untitled
(1909, after visiting Gettysburg as a West Point cadet)

The brave went down
   Without disgrace they leaped to ruin's red embrace.
They only heard fame's thunder wake
   And saw the dazzling sun burst break
      In smiles on glory's bloody face.

A Toast
(1903-5, at West Point)

Oh! here's to the snarl of the striving steel
   When eye met eye on the foughten field.
And the life went out with the entering steel
   In the days when war was war.

After World War I, Army Col. George Patton remained in France to learn more about tank warfare. Here he stands in front of a Renault behemoth at Bourg, France in 1918. During the Great War and on into World War II, Patton maintained a journal and wrote numerous poems, revealing a compassionate side that few ever saw. (U.S. Army)

And here's to the men who fought and strove,
    And parried and hacked and thrust and clove
Who fought for honor and fought for love
    In the days when war was war.

Oh! here's to the maids for whom they fought.
    For whom they strove, of whom they thought.
The maids whose love they nobly sought,
    In the days when war was war.

The Curse of Kant
(1917)

The papers publish sob-stuff
    and drool of the horrors of strife
They speak of the fallen as murdered
    and lie about us and our life.

But we who are in it know better
    There still is a glory to war
The death which one dies for Country
    Is nobler than ever before.

The wolf which fights not for her litter
    The man who resents not a blow
The nation which makes mock of glory
    Shall perish in limitless woe.

Men who have struggled as heroes
    Men who have suffered and bled
Men who have frozen and hungered
    Should be honored, living or dead.

But ours who have prated of ethics
    and cringed at the sufferings of strife

Dishonor their land and their women
    and the pains which have given them life.

The youth who dies for his country
    But follows the teachings of God
Giving life that others may prosper
    He treads as his Savior trod.

Then seek not in maudlin pity
    To regret those nobly slain
Who die in their land's service
    Have never lived in vain.

For those whose lives are spent in lust
    Of ease or wealth or food
Whose souls have rotted e'er they died
    Whose deaths have done no good.

For such set up your woeful howls
    For such pour forth your prayers
The brave who dies needs not your sighs
    Nor for your pity cares.

Let papers cease to mourn the lost
    Mourn fights we do not gain
Instead of mulling o'er the dead
    Enlist! Replace the slain.

A Code of Action
(1917, while establishing a tank training
center in Langres, France)

I didn't begin with askings
    I took my job and stuck
I took the chances they wouldn't
    and now they are calling it luck.

In wondrous catlike ability
    For grasping all things which go by
To land on my feet with agility
    No one is greater than I.

In doing the things others will not
    In standing the blows others shirk
In grasping the chance that returns not
    and never yet shirking my work.

For these gifts, Oh! God, I thank Thee
    Pray let me continue the same
Since, by doing things well which are nearest
    Perhaps I shall yet rise to fame.

It is not in intricate planning
    Nor yet in regretting the past
That great men whose lives we are watching
    Have gained to their greatness at last.

Hence praise we the just mead of striving
    Which foolish make light of as luck
There never was yet luck in shirking
    While much is accomplished through pluck.

So seize I the things which are nearest
    and studious fall on my feet
Do ever in all things my damndest
    and never, Oh, never retreat!

Bill
(1918, in tribute to a 304th Brigade tank crew)

Bill, he kept racin' the motor,
    for fear that the damned thing would die.

While I fiddled 'round with the breech block
    and wished for a piece of your pie.

It's funny the way it affects you,
    When you're waitin' for the signal to go.
There's none of the high moral feeling
    About which the newspapers blow.

For myself, I always is hungry,
    While Bill thought his spark plugs was foul.
Some guys talks o' sprees they has been on,
    and one kid, what's croaked, thought of school.

At last, I seen Number One signal;
    I beat on the back o' Bill's neck.
He slipped her the juice and she started,
    and Bill he ain't never come back.

The first news we had of the Boches
    Was shot splinters, right in the eye.
I cussed twice as loud as the Colonel,
    and forgot all about the old pie.

A Boche he runs out with a tank gun;
    I gave him H.E. in the guts.
You ought to have seen him pop open!
    They sure was well fed, was them sluts.

We wiped out two nests with case shot,
    and was just gettin' into a third,
When we plunked in a hole full of water.
    That God-d— Bill sure was a bird.

He hollers, "Frank, you're married;
    If only one gets out, it's you."

and he rammed me up out of the turret . . .
    I guess that's about all I knew.

A stinkin' whizz-bang beaned me,
    Or I might of rescued Bill,
But it's too late now. He's sleepin'
    By our tank, on that God-d— hill.

They gave him a Medal of Honor,
    For savin' me for you,
So if it's a boy we'll name it Bill,
    It's the least and the most we can do.

Valor
(1915, in response to Pres. Woodrow Wilson's
declaration of neutrality)

When all hearts are opened,
    and all the secrets known,
When guile and lies are banished,
    and subterfuge is gone.

When God rolls up the curtain,
    and hidden truths appear,
When the ghastly light of Judgment Day,
    Brings past and present near . . .

Then shall we know what once we knew,
    Before wealth dimmed our sight,
That of all sins, the blackest is
    The pride which will not fight.

The meek and pious have a place,
    and necessary are,
But valor pales their puny rays,
    As does the sun a star.

What race of men since time began,
    Has ever yet remained,
Who trusted not its own right hand,
    Or from brave deeds refrained?

Yet spite the fact for ages known,
    and by all lands displayed,
We still have those who prate of peace,
    and say that war is dead.

Yes vandals rise who seek to snatch
    The laurels from the brave,
and dare defame heroic dead,
    Now filling hero graves.

They speak of those who love,
    Like Christ's, exceeds the lust of life
and murderers slain to no avail,
    A useless sacrifice.

With infamy without a name,
    They mock our fighting youth,
and dare decry great hearts who die,
    Battling for right and truth.

Woe to the land which, heeding them,
    Lets avarice gain the day,
and trusting gold it's right to hold,
    Lets manly might decay.

Let us, while willing yet for peace,
    Still keep our valor high,
So when our time of battle comes,
    We shall not fear to die.

Make love of life and ease be less,
　Make love of country more.
So shall our patriotism be
　More than an empty roar.

For death is nothing, comfort less,
　Valor is all in all;
Base nations who depart from it,
　Shall sure and justly fall.

In addition to studying previous battles over the same terrain he would soon be dispatching his troops to conquer, General Patton relied on feedback from his forward commanders, to assess and respond quicker than any of his counterparts. Near Brolo, Sicily in 1943, Patton (left) talked with Thirtieth Infantry Regiment commander Lt. Col. Lyle Bernard, for an assessment of the advance toward Messina. (U.S. Army)

Chapter 9

Views on War

As a boy, George Patton was influenced by medieval tales of knights and dragons and damsels in distress, by Nordic myths of sailing turbulent seas to the edge of the world and conquering unheard-of evils and distant lands. As he matured and prepared to become a great commander in his own right, he studied Prussian militarism, specifically Marshal Helmuth von Moltke, who advanced a divine view of war suggesting that civilizations would actually thrive on upheaval. Prior to the Allied invasion of North Africa, Patton read the Koran to better understand Arab thinking, and he often turned to his Bible for solace and guidance. These were just a few of his many influences. He had not only read about the great armies and their bold commanders but could also recite lengthy passages from their writings. He followed in their footsteps over some of the same territories they conquered in centuries past. He would write in his journal in October 1943, "I could almost picture in my mind's eye the small groups of knights and men-at-arms who, by virtue of occupying these strong points, ruled the world as they knew it, and how pitifully weak in numbers and armor they were in comparison with our guns, tanks and infantry, which rolled by them in endless streams."

"Despite the oceans of ink and years of thought which have been devoted to the elucidation of war, its secrets still remain shrouded in mystery. Indeed, it is due largely to the very volume of available information that the veil is so thick.

"War is an art and as such it is not susceptible to explanation by fixed formulae. Yet, from the earliest time there has been an unending effort to subject its complex and emotional structure to dissection, to enunciate rules for its waging, to make tangible its intangibility. One might as well attempt to isolate the soul by the dissection of a cadaver as to seek the essence of war by the analysis of its records."

"Magnificent! Compared to war, all other forms of human endeavor shrink to insignificance. God help me, I do love it so!"
~ *Patton responding to an artillery barrage in France, July-August 1944.*

"It is hard to answer intelligently the question, 'Why I want to be a soldier.' For my own satisfaction I have tried to give myself reasons but have never found any logical ones. I only feel that it is inside me. It is as natural for me to be a soldier as it is to breathe and would be as hard to give up all thought of being a soldier as it would be to stop breathing."

"I believe that for a man to become a great soldier it is necessary for him to be so thoroughly conversant with all sorts of military possibilities that whenever an occasion arises, he has at hand, without effort on his part, a parallel.

"To attain this end, I believe that it is necessary for a man to begin to read military history in its earliest and crudest form and to follow it down in natural sequence, permitting his mind to grow with his subject until he can grasp, without any effort, the most abstract question of the Science of War because he is already permeated with its elements."

"Through the murk of fact and fable rises to our view this one truth: the history of war is the history of warriors; few in number but mighty in influence.

"Alexander, not Macedonia, conquered the world.

"Scipio, not Rome, destroyed Carthage.

"Marlborough, not the Allies, defeated France.

"Cromwell, not the Roundheads, dethroned Charles."

"I am not a brilliant soldier. So far, I have been quite successful because I am always fully confident that I can do what must be done and have had my sense of duty developed to the point where I let no personal interests or danger interfere."

"Personally, I am of the opinion that older men of experience, who have smelled powder and have been wounded, are of more value than mere youthful exuberance, which has not yet been disciplined. However, I seem to be in the minority in this belief."

"When a surgeon decides in the course of an operation to change its objective, to splice that artery or cut deeper and remove another organ which he finds infected, he is not making a snap decision, but one based on years of knowledge, experience and training. It is the same with professional soldiers."

Before going into battle, General Patton believed in studying his opponent for strengths, weaknesses, tendencies, and vulnerabilities. He also read the historical record of previous campaigns in the same region.

During the push across France, Patton lugged along the six-volume set of the *History of the Norman Conquest,* by

British historian Edward Freeman. Later, as he moved across Northern Europe, he read a book written by the one enemy commander many considered his equal—Erwin Rommel, who wrote *Infantry Attacks*, which revealed the field marshal's combat experiences in World War I.

These two respected tacticians studied and respected each other. Rommel would remark, "We had to wait until the Patton Army was in France to see the most astonishing achievements in mobile warfare." Patton relished nothing better than the idea of taking on Rommel, man to man, tank versus tank, anytime, anywhere. It would be a duel to the death, winner take all. Everyone else could simply watch. But they never actually faced one another.

"I have studied the German all of my life. I have read the memoirs of his generals and political leaders. I have even read his philosophers and listened to his music. I have studied in detail the accounts of every damned one of his battles. I know exactly how he will react under any given set of circumstances. He hasn't the slightest idea of what I'm going to do. Therefore, when the time comes, I'm going to whip the Hell out of him."

"American soldiers are most ingenious. When they could not capture a town to sleep in, they would roll three large snowballs or snow rolls, place one on each side and the third on the windward end, and, lining them with pine tree branches, they slept in groups of three or four. How human beings could endure this continuous fighting at sub-zero temperatures is still beyond my comprehension." ~ *Journal entry, January 29 to March 12, 1945*.

"Julius Caesar would have a tough time being a Brigadier General in my Army."

"Looking over the country where we fought during the battle of El Guettar gives one a definite idea of the greatness of the American soldier. The mountains are impossibly difficult. Had I known how difficult it was, I might have been less bold—but it is always well to remember that the country is just as hard on the enemy as it is on you." ~ *Journal entry, Malta, December 19, 1943.*

—⊷—

"I consider it no sacrifice to die for my country. In my mind, we came here to thank God that men like these have lived rather than to regret that they have died."

—⊷—

The United States and Russia were allies in defeating Nazi Germany, and everyone smiled for the cameras when they linked up at the Elbe River in the final weeks of the war. George Patton's juggernaut known as the Third Army was clearly the more potent force, but they were ordered to halt their advance so Russian forces could capture Berlin, thus ending Adolf Hitler's Thousand-Year Reich.

However, Patton was aware that Josef Stalin was just as much a ruthless dictator as Hitler. So he wanted to attack Berlin and kill "that Nazi bastard," then keep right on going, all the way to Moscow to rid the world of Stalin too:

"Tin soldier politicians in Washington have allowed us to kick the Hell out of one bastard and at the same time forced us to help establish a second one as evil or more evil than the first. . . .

"This time we'll need almighty God's constant help if we're to live in the same world with Stalin and his murdering cutthroats."

—⊷—

"Let's keep our boots polished, bayonets sharpened and

present a picture of force and strength to the Russians. This is the only language that they understand and respect. If you fail to do this, then I would like to say that we have had a victory over the Germans, and have disarmed them, but we have lost the war." ~ *Patton to Undersecretary of War Robert Porter Patterson, May 6, 1945.*

Chapter 10

On Rapid Advance

The Nazis heard of Patton's larger-than-life war-fighting reputation before witnessing his swashbuckling tactics, in North Africa, Sicily, France, and on into Germany. Some called it a juggernaut or steamroller or even whispered that his bold maneuvers bested their own blitzkrieg tactics. But whatever they dubbed it, and whatever they attempted in desperation to stop it, the German army—the *Wehrmacht*—failed to check the Patton tidal wave in every confrontation. In many cases they could not even slow it down. In mid-1944 Patton wrote in his journal, "I even had a slight feeling of sympathy for the Germans, who must now have known that the attack they had been fearing had at last arrived. I complacently remembered that I had always 'Demanded the Impossible,' that I had 'Dared extreme occasion,' and that I had 'Not taken counsel of my fears.'"

His philosophy was very simple: *"L'audace, l'audace, toujours l'audace."* ("Audacity, audacity, always audacity.") Patton expected his units to advance, no matter what the obstacles might be. Advance—no excuses—*advance*.

His soldiers were young. Initially they were scared and all wanted to be somewhere other than where they were, about to go into battle. But they believed in Patton. They knew what had to be done and knew it required brutality and swiftness.

After surviving the horrors and miseries of trench warfare during World War I, George Patton became a proponent of the theory of rapid advance. Nazi Germany first unleashed this lightning-war or blitzkrieg tactic when their Condor Legion fought in Spain. They later stunned the world when they steamrolled over Poland with little resistance, in September of 1939. And of course, Patton became aware of Germany's battlefield successes across Europe. Sensing that it was only a matter of time before the United States was pulled into the fighting, he drilled his units at every opportunity in this new tactic. Here, at the Desert Training Center in California, he stands beside an M3 Stuart tank while reading a compass. (Patton Museum)

They also knew that fear and hesitation only increased their casualty count. Patton had them believing that it was better for the other guys to die for their country . . . as soon as possible. He hammered that point home, at every opportunity.

"Every soldier should realize that casualties in battle are the result of two factors: first, effective enemy fire, and second, the time during which the soldier is exposed to that fire. The enemy's effectiveness in fire is reduced by your fire or by night attacks. The time you are exposed is reduced by the rapidity of your advance." ~ *Journal entry.*

"There is only one tactical principle which is not subject to change. It is, 'To use the means at hand to inflict the maximum amount of wounds, death and destruction on the enemy in the minimum amount of time.'" ~ *Patton in Third United States Army Letter of Instruction Number 2, April 3, 1944.*

"Infantry must move forward to close with the enemy. It must shoot in order to move. . . . To halt under fire is folly. To halt under fire and not fire back is suicide. Officers must set the example." ~ *Patton in Third United States Army Letter of Instruction Number 2, April 3, 1944.*

"A tank which stops to fire, gets hit."

"People must try to use their imagination. When orders fail to come they must act on their own best judgment. A very safe rule to follow is that in case of doubt, push on a little further and then keep on pushing."

Patton's brilliance on the battlefield was marked by this proven tactic of rapid advance, often cutting off or overwhelming enemy forces before they could react. But the typical role of infantry soldiers—the "ground-pounders" trudging from one battle to the next—would only hinder the forward rush Patton envisioned. Instead, he wanted his soldiers to ride into battle, on anything that moved forward.

"When, early in the campaign, I had issued orders that at least one regimental combat team of infantry should ride on the tanks of an armored division, the 5th Infantry Division complained most bitterly, stating, among other things, that there was nothing for the men to hold on to. I told them that was the men's hard luck, but I was sure soldiers would rather ride on anything for 25 miles than walk 15 miles," Patton would write in his journal in mid-1944.

"In a modern infantry division, if every available vehicle— tanks, armored cars, gun carriages, AA guns and trucks—is utilized, no soldier need or should walk until he actually enters battle. While the sight of a division moving under this system is abhorrent to the best instincts of a Frederickan soldier, it results in rapid advance with minimum fatigue." ~ *Journal entry.*

"Use steamroller strategy; that is, make up your mind on course and direction of action and stick to it. But in tactics, do not steamroller. Attack weakness. Hold them by the nose and kick them in the a–." ~ *Journal entry, November 2, 1942.*

"A good plan violently executed right now is far better than a perfect plan executed next week."

Advancing on the enemy was always a perilous task and

General Patton was adamant that his units not allow terrain to dictate their avenue of approach. In fact, he stated, "it is much better to go over difficult ground where you are not expected than it is over good ground where you are."

"In battle, the soldier enters a lottery with death as the stake. The only saving clauses in this gamble lie in time and the demoralizing effect produced on the enemy by the rapid and uninterrupted advance of the attacker."

Despite being called Old Blood and Guts, the last thing Patton wanted was a high casualty count among his men. He knew that there was a direct correlation between rapid advance and minimal losses. So he constantly badgered his commanders to maintain the offensive, to take on the enemy with brutality, ruthlessness, and no room for compassion.

"We can conquer only by attacking."

"Speed and ruthless violence on the beaches is vital. There must be no hesitation in debarking. To linger on the beaches is fatal."

During the Civil War, Ulysses S. Grant said, "In every battle there comes a time when both sides consider themselves beaten, then he who continues the attack wins." At Chancellorsville, his opponent, Robert E. Lee, said something similar: "I was too weak to defend, so I attacked."

Both of these comments from two old warhorses of American history were recalled by General Patton when his forces were stalled near Nancy in France. Later, though surrounded by Nazi forces who demanded they surrender, the Battling Bastards of Bastogne refused to give up. They chose to fight on, until Patton's reinforcements could burst through the lines and drive off the Nazi attackers.

"Death in battle is a function of time. The longer troops remain under fire, the more men get killed. Therefore, everything must be done to speed up movement." ~ *Patton to officers and men of the Forty-Fifth Division in England, June 27, 1944.*

"The fierce frenzy of hate and determination flashing from the bloodshot eyes squinting behind the glittering steel is what wins wars."

"You don't have to hurry; you have to run like hell."

"In case of doubt, *attack!*"

Chapter 11

War Poems

The American Expeditionary Force, led by Gen. John Black Jack Pershing, was sent to Europe to bolster Allied forces in World War I. George Patton was a hard-charging junior officer, itching for action, yearning to experience what he dreamed of as a boy. Much of what he saw and experienced in the Great War was documented in his many cryptic but brutally graphic war poems.

L'Envoi
(1916)

When the last great battle is finished
   and the last great general shall fall,
When the roar of the mighty guns is dumb
   as the kiss of the nickeled ball.

When the screams of the dying that mixed
    With the shout that the living give out
      As they rush on the foe,
When the mixed noise of an army in flight
    The gasp and the curse and the shouting are low,
When soldiers have ceased to struggle,
    When war is raged with the tongue,

By leading from the front, George Patton was able to assess and change the course of a battle without the critical delays experienced by many of his counterparts, who made their decisions well to the rear, far removed from danger. More than too often, though, enemy soldiers fired at him as he roamed close to the frontlines. Many of Patton's war poems reveal this sense of danger and the thrill of cheating death. Here he watches bridging operations over the Sauer River, on February 20, 1945. (Patton Museum)

When men are praised for cowardice
   And men for bravery hung,

When honor and virtue and courage
   Are fled like departing day
As the cursed shape of eternal peace
   Comes up on the evening gray,

When money is God and Lord of all
   and liars alone have weight,
When the road to heaven is barred with gold
   and wide yawns Hell's black gate—

Then those who live in servile chains
   To filthy lucre slaves
Ah, how they will yearn for the soldier's life
   and for the hero's grave, and will say as they sadly think of it:
      War was a priceless benefit, although a sacrifice.

The Precious Babies
(1918)

Up and down the roadways, through the German ranks,
   Nosing out machine guns, come the baby tanks.
Scrambling through the crater, splashing through the pool,
   Like the Usher's happy boys, bounding out of school.

Fritz is great on wirefields, trust the Boche for that,
   But his choicest efforts fall extremely flat.
Wasted in the weaving of laborious days,
   When the merry infant class scampers through the maze.

Cheerful little children of an American brain,
   Winning ravished country back to France again.
On thru town and village, shepherded by Yanks
   Romping, blithe and rollicking, roll the baby tanks.

Through a Glass, Darkly
(1922)

Through the travail of the ages, midst the pomp and toil of war,
    Have I fought and strove and perished countless times upon
        this star.
In the form of many people, in all panoplies of time
    Have I seen the luring vision of the Victory Maid, sublime.

I have battled for fresh mammoth, I have warred for pastures new,
    I have listed to the whispers when the race trek instinct grew.
I have known the call to battle, in each changeless changing shape
    From the high souled voice of conscience to the beastly lust
        for rape.

I have sinned and I have suffered, played the hero and the knave;
    Fought for belly, shame, or country and for each have found
        a grave.
I cannot name my battles, for the visions are not clear,
    Yet, I see the twisted faces and I feel the rending spear.

Perhaps I stabbed our Savior in His sacred helpless side.
    Yet, I've called His name in blessing when after times I died.
In the dimness of the shadows, where we hairy heathens warred,
    I can taste in thought the lifeblood; we used teeth before
        the sword.

While in later clearer vision I can sense the coppery sweat,
    Feel the pikes grow wet and slippery, when our Phalanx,
        Cyrus met.
Hear the rattle of the harness, where the Persian darts
        bounced clear,
    See their chariots wheel in panic, from the Hoplite's leveled
        spear.

See the goal grow monthly longer, reaching for the walls of Tyre.
   Hear the crash of tons of granite, smell the quenchless
     eastern fire.
Still more clearly as a Roman, can I see the Legion close,
   As our third rank moved in forward and the short sword
     found our foes.

Once again I feel the anguish of that blistering treeless plain
   When the Parthian showered death bolts, and our discipline
     was in vain.
I remember all the suffering of those arrows in my neck.
   Yet, I stabbed a grinning savage as I died upon my back.

Once again I smell the heat sparks, when my flemish plate
     gave way
   and the lance ripped through my entrails as on Crecy's field
     I lay.
In the windless, blinding stillness of the glittering tropic sea
   I can see the bubbles rising where we set the captives free.

Midst the spume of half a tempest, I have heard the bulwarks go
   When the crashing, point blank round shot sent destruction
     to our foe.
I have fought with gun and cutlass on the red and slippery deck
   With all Hell aflame within me and a rope around my neck.

And still later as a General have I galloped with Murat
   When we laughed at death and numbers, trusting in the
     Emperor's Star.
Till at last our star faded, and we shouted to our doom
   Where the sunken road of Ohein closed us in its quivering
     gloom.

So but now with Tanks a'clatter have I waddled on the foe
   Belching death at twenty paces, by the star shell's ghastly glow.

So as through a glass, and darkly the age long strife I see
    Where I fought in many guises, many names—but always me.

And I see not in my blindness what the objects were I wrought,
    But as God rules o'er our bickering, it was through His will
        I fought.
So forever in the future, shall I battle as of yore,
    Dying to be born a fighter, but to die again, once more.

Two decades later, General Patton's poems about his World War II experiences are graphically brutal and intensely personal, conveying his feelings about the moment that prompted him to rip open a vein and bleed on his private papers.

His verses may not be able to withstand the harsh glare of literary critique, but they do reveal small glimpses of this complex man who exuded surliness and rarely displayed his softer side.

"Seven Up" refers to the mighty Seventh Army and its five-week Sicily campaign. Soon after, Patton was removed from command for slapping two soldiers he felt were feigning cowardice in field hospitals. While writing this poem, he felt that one day he would once again lead the Seventh to more conquests. Instead, he would head up the Third Army in the final battles of Fortress Europe.

Seven Up
(1943)

Once there was an Army, then one day it died.
    So tell the bell and waken Hell, to give it room inside.
The story of this Army is very, very drear
    Its beginning and its ending were especially queer.

They made its chief a permanent so he perchance could wave
    At others hurrying past him their country for to save.

But now just like a skeleton upon the desert floor
  Orders like vultures come each day to pick away some more.

The thing has got so very bad that now his friends suspect
  That he no longer can command even his self-respect.
Yet like the fabled Phoenix the Seventh shall arise
  Again to soar in triumph through flaming smoke veiled skies.

God of Battles
(1943)

From pride and foolish confidence, from every weakening creed,
  From the dread fear of fearing, protect us, Lord and lead.

Great God, who, through the ages, has braced the bloodstained
    hand,
  As Saturn, Jove, or Woden has led our Warrior band.

Again we seek thy counsel, but not in cringing guise,
  We whine not for thy mercy, to slay; God make us wise.

For slaves who shun the issue, who do not ask thy aid,
  To Thee we trust our spirits, our bodies, unafraid.

From doubt and fearsome boding, still Thou our spirits guard,
  Make strong our souls to conquer. Give us the victory, Lord.

———

The brutality of warfare is in direct opposition to the lyricism of poetry, as though the instigator of one could not be the creator of the other. In the select company of warriors, the poet is denounced as a man who avoids the physical deprivations of battle, so how to explain George Patton, the Spartan warrior, the student of military history, the brilliant tactician, the battle-scarred poet?

In mid-August of 1944, as he prepared to unleash his

ground forces on the Nazi defenders of Fortress Europe, Patton wrote "Absolute War," which conveyed his exasperation with the plodding, methodical battle tactics of his rival Allied commanders, most notably the British.

Absolute War
(1944)

Now in war we are confronted with conditions which are strange.
    If we accept them we will never win.
Since by being realistic, as in mundane combats fistic,
    We will get a bloody nose and that's a sin.

To avoid such fell disaster, the result of fighting faster,
    We resort to fighting carefully and slow.
We fill up terrestrial spaces with secure expensive bases
    To keep our tax rate high and death rate low.

But with sadness and with sorrow we discover to our horror
    That while we build, the enemy gets set.
So despite our fine intentions to produce extensive pensions
    We haven't licked the dirty bastard yet.

For in war just as in loving, you must always keep on shoving
    Or you'll never get your just reward.
For if you are dilatory in the search for lust and glory
    You are up s— creek and that's the truth, Oh! Lord.

So let us do real fighting, boring in and gouging, biting.
    Let's take a chance now that we have the ball.
Let's forget those fine firm bases in the dreary shell raked spaces.
    Let's shoot the works and win! Yes, win it all!

———

For several decades George Patton had read about all the great battles in history, imagining he was at each. In World

Wars I and II, he was always near the front, exposed to danger, as if he was yearning for the glorious death that befell so many other great commanders, securing their legacy for all time. Yet war is ugly, and Patton made no attempt to sanitize the ugliness he saw over his many years in combat.

Fear
(1920)

I am that dreadful, blighting thing, like rat holes to the flood.
   Like rust that gnaws the faultless blade, like microbes to the blood.
I know no mercy and no truth, the young I blight, the old I slay.
   Regret stalks darkly in my wake, and ignominy dogs my way.

Sometimes, in virtuous garb I rove, with facile talk of easier way;
   Seducing where I dare not rape, young manhood from its honor's sway.
Again, in awesome guise I rush, stupendous, through the ranks of war,
   Turning to water, with my gaze, hearts that, before, no foe could awe.

The maiden who has strayed from right, to me must pay the mead of shame.
   The patriot who betrays his trust, to me must owe his tarnished name.
I spare no class, nor cult, nor creed, my course is endless through the year.
   I bow all heads and break all hearts, all owe me homage—I am *fear.*

Col. Chauncy Benson was an old World War I ally of George Patton. During the fighting in Tunisia, Benson's unit became lost and bogged down in a minefield. "He hollered in the

608" refers to an old army field telephone and "G-2" is army intelligence. "Jebyl" is a combination of *djebel* (hill in Arabic) and "devil." During the North African battle of El Guettar, Djebel Chemsi and Djebel Ben Kreir were important hills appearing on battle maps.

That Must Be Benson
(1943)

The forward observer clearly saw
   Thirteen tanks in a wadi draw.
"Help" he hollered in the 608
   "Shoot 'em now or it'll be too late.

"At five thousand yards I can't be wrong—
   They look too low and they look too long."
Up jumped the General and he said, said he
   "Where in the Jebyl can Benson be?"

"Benson, boys," the G-2 said,
   "Tells me daily where he means to head.
"Today is usual, and he's never late,
   He's smack on grid-line Thirty-Eight."

So Reap reported without delay
   "Battalion, three rounds, on the way."
Then up bounced Benson, and he said, said he,
   "Whose in the Jebyl can those rounds be?"

Buzz went the phone and buzz went the wire
   And buzz went my ear with a loud "Cease fire!"
"I know blame well," said the voice, "this party
   can't be Jerry . . . it's Irwin's Army."

"Now Chauncy," said the General, half irate,
   "Aren't you fighting this out on Thirty-Eight?"

"Our fire's at fifty," said Benson, "ah, me.
   "Where in the Jebyl can Three Eight be?"

A Soldier's Prayer
(1944)

God of our Father, who by land and sea
   has ever led us on to victory,
      please continue your inspiring guidance
   in this greatest of our conflicts.

Strengthen my soul so that the weakening instinct
   of self preservation, which besets all of us in battle,
      shall not blind me to my duty to my own manhood,
   to the Glory of my calling,
      and to my responsibility to my Fellow soldiers.

Grant to our Armed Forces that disciplined valor
   and mutual confidence which insures success in war.
Let me not mourn for the men who have died fighting,
   but rather let me be glad that such heroes have lived.

If it be my lot to die, let me do so with courage
   and honor in a manner which will bring
      the greatest harm to the enemy,
   and please, oh Lord, protect and guide those
      I shall leave behind. Give us victory, Lord.

Patton had little tolerance for the slow, methodical strategy of advance employed by British forces commanded by Field Marshal Bernard Montgomery. In fact, Patton and Monty despised each other and frequently played the silly game of one-upsmanship. Here Patton, Omar Bradley, and Monty chat in France on July 7, 1944. (Army Signal Corps)

Chapter 12

On the Role of Commanders

General Patton studied warfare and the commanders who directed it, including Alexander the Great and Julius Caesar, Ulysses Grant and Robert E. Lee. He learned that William Tecumseh Sherman believed in leading from the front, where he could redirect his forces as events unfolded. In his *Memoirs*, Sherman wrote, "Some men think that modern armies may be so regulated that a general can sit in an office and play on his several columns as on the keys of a piano; this is a fearful mistake. Every attempt to make war easy and safe will result in humiliation and disaster." Throwing caution to the wind at every opportunity, George Patton could not be an "armchair general" and was highly critical of those who were, including several prominent Allied commanders in World War II.

―――

"There is a great deal of talk about loyalty from the bottom to the top. Loyalty from the top down is even more necessary and is much less prevalent. One of the most frequently noted characteristics of great men who have remained great is loyalty to their subordinates."

―――

"The leader must be an actor. He is unconvincing unless he lives the part. The fixed determination to acquire the 'Warrior Soul' and having acquired it, to conquer or perish with honor is the secret of victory."

———

"The greatest gift a general can have is a bad temper. A bad temper gives you a sort of divine wrath and it is only by the use of a divine wrath that you can drive men beyond their physical ability in order to save their lives."

———

"I have a notion that usually the great things a man does appear to be great only after we have passed them. When they are at hand they are normal decisions and are done without knowledge. In the case of a General, for example, the almost superhuman knowledge which he is supposed to possess exists only in the mind of his biographer."

———

"A piece of spaghetti or a military unit can only be led from the front end."

———

"Be willing to make decisions. That's the most important quality in a good leader."

———

"Wars may be fought with weapons, but they are won by men. It is the spirit of the men who follow and the man who leads that gains victory."

———

"The time to take counsel of your fears is before you make an important battle decision. That's the time to listen to every fear you can imagine! When you have collected all the facts and fears and made your decision, turn off all your fears and go ahead!"

―――

"If you can't get them to salute when they should salute and wear the clothes you tell them to wear, how are you going to get them to die for their country?"

―――

"In any war, a commander, no matter what his rank, has to send to certain death, nearly every day, by his own orders, a certain number of men. Some are his personal friends. All are his personal responsibility; to them as his troops and to their families.

"Any man with a heart would like to sit down and bawl like a baby, but he can't. So, he sticks out his jaw and swaggers and swears. I wish some of those pious sob sisters at home could understand something as basic as that."

―――

"It is better to live in the limelight for a year than in the wings forever."

―――

"All very successful commanders are prima donnas and must be so treated."

―――

"Commanding an army is not such a very absorbing task except that one must be ready at all hours of the day and night to make some momentous decision, which frequently consists of telling somebody who thinks that he is beaten that he is not beaten."

―――

"It is really amazing what the determination on the part of one man can do to many thousands."

―――

"Success in war depends on the 'golden rules of war'—speed, simplicity, and boldness."

When preparing his soldiers for battle, George Patton knew that some of them wouldn't make it, and he told them so. But he also expected every one of them to face down their fears and give it their all, without hesitation. "Kill devastatingly . . . die valiantly," he would tell them. If it must be so, then there is no greater glory than to die in battle. (Patton Museum)

Chapter 13

On Courage Under Fire

George Patton was onboard the warship USS *Augusta* and as it approached the coastal waters of North Africa, he issued orders to his troops of the Western Task Force—35,000 strong—prior to kicking off Operation Torch. He would make several beach landings during World War II, from North Africa to Sicily and Anzio, reminding Patton of past conquests. He wrote in his journal in October 1943, "The city and harbor of Syracuse are to me of particular interest because this place probably has been the scene of more amphibious operations than any other harbor in the world. When looking over its water I could almost see the Greek triremes, the Roman galleys, the Vandals, the Arabs, the Crusaders, the French, the English and the Americans, who, to mention only a few, have successively stormed, or attempted to storm, that harbor." But the North Africa campaign was the first for America's untested men in uniform. No one knew what to expect, especially with three separate factions of French forces (neutral, pro-Nazi, and pro-Allied) mixed in with Germany's battle-tested Afrika Korps.

"We are now on our way to force a landing on the coast of Northwest Africa. We are to be congratulated because we have been chosen as the units of the United States Army to take part in this great American effort.

"Our mission is threefold. First to capture a beachhead, second to capture the city of Casablanca, third to move against the German wherever he may be and destroy him. We may be opposed by a limited number of Germans. It is not known whether the French Army will contest our landing. It is regrettable to contemplate the necessity of fighting the gallant French, who are at heart sympathetic, but all resistance, by whomever offered, must be destroyed." ~ *Patton's orders to his troops.*

———

"This war makes higher demands on courage and discipline than any war of which I have known. But, when you see men who have demonstrated discipline and courage, killed and wounded, it naturally raises a lump in your throat and sometimes produces a tear in your eye."

———

The skies over Casablanca were lit up with searchlights probing the darkness for enemy and Allied planes roaring overhead. Onboard transport planes from England were paratroopers who would be dropped behind the lines as part of Operation Torch. General Patton and his landing force were farther out at sea, observing the spectacle and waiting for the green light to storm ashore. He and his aides had been preparing to board his landing craft slung on the side of the *Augusta* when French destroyers confronted the Allied task force and began firing. During the exchange of fire, the landing craft, with all of Patton's personal belongings onboard, ended up in the drink. The *Augusta* went in full pursuit of the French tormentors, with Patton helplessly, impatiently observing this naval engagement and wanting to get ashore, where his ground forces were already engaged at Fedala's Red Beach.

After the North Africa campaign, it was on to Sicily.

———

"The last stand was made in the mountains southwest of Palermo, which was a most difficult nut to crack, but was finally done with artillery fire and tanks. As we approached, the hills on each side were burning. We then started down a long road cut out of the side of a cliff which went through an almost continuous village. The street was full of people shouting, 'Down with Mussolini!' and 'Long Live America.'

"When we got into the town, the same thing went on. Those who arrived before dark had flowers thrown on the road in front of them, and lemons and watermelons given them in such profusion that they almost became lethal weapons." ~ *Journal entry, July 23, 1943.*

———

"Soldiers of the Seventh Army: Born at sea, baptized in blood and crowned with victory, in the course of 38 days of incessant battle and unceasing labor, you have added a glorious chapter to the history of war." ~ *Patton to his soldiers of the Seventh Army, August 22, 1943.*

———

In *As You Like It,* Shakespeare wrote, "Then a soldier, full of strange oaths and bearded like the pard,/Jealous in honour, sudden and quick in quarrel, seeking the bubble reputation, even in the cannon's mouth . . . " General Patton knew many soldiers and even officers who said they experienced combat, without putting themselves in real danger. Others were so desperate for heroism that they exposed themselves to needless enemy fire, thus the "bubble reputation."

"It is an unfortunate and, to me, tragic fact that in our attempts to prevent war we have taught our people to belittle the heroic qualities of the soldier. They do not realize that, as

Shakespeare put it, the pursuit of 'the bubble reputation even at the cannon's mouth' is not only a good military characteristic but also very helpful to the young man when bullets and shells are whistling and crackling around him." ~ *Journal entry.*

———

"It is only by doing things others have not that one can advance."

———

"We are ready. I shall be delighted to lead you men against any enemy. I am confident that your disciplined valor and high training will bring victory."

———

During the months leading up to D-Day, General Patton commanded the fictitious Fortitude South task force in southern England, complete with dummy tanks, rubber artillery pieces, and flimsy landing craft and harbor equipment that looked very real to Nazi spies and surveillance planes watching from a distance. Thousands of Allied soldiers were being held in reserve to dupe the enemy into thinking that the Allies' most-feared commander was heading up Armegruppe Patton, the main invasion force.

Message traffic from Patton's headquarters was "intercepted" by Nazi radio operators, and plenty of intentionally released info made it all the way to Berlin. It all indicated a full-scale invasion of France at Calais, just twenty miles from the cliffs at Dover. The bulk of the Nazis waited in Calais to obliterate Patton's forces. (Even when Allied forces stormed ashore at Normandy, the Nazis still believed it was a feint and the real invasion would be spearheaded by Patton, at Calais.)

By the end of May, Patton visited all of his units and spoke to every soldier, giving them the following pep talk, with slight variations:

General Patton's Address to the Troops Before the Commencement of Operation Overlord. Somewhere in England

Men, this stuff that some sources sling around about America wanting out of this war, not wanting to fight, is a crock of bulls—.

Americans love to fight, traditionally. All real Americans love the sting and clash of battle. You are here today for three reasons. First, because you are here to defend your homes and your loved ones. Second, you are here for your own self respect, because you would not want to be anywhere else. Third, you are here because you are real men and all real men like to fight.

———

Though he was held out of the initial assault on Fortress Europe, George Patton wasted little time once he joined the battle. As he directed his troops across France and northern Europe, he knew he was traversing territory that had been conquered by the Romans, Huns, Charles, Napoleon, and his own mentor, Black Jack Pershing. Patton studied these past conquests to assure his own victories in 1944 and '45.

On many occasions, Patton told others he had been at battles that had occurred in past centuries, hinting that he believed in reincarnation. After the Ninety-Fourth Division took over Saarburg in Germany, in late February of 1945, he recalled that the former king of Bohemia, John the Blind, had occupied the castle there. He died in 1346 during the war between the French and the English. Patton would later say to his daughter, "I was there" to witness the demise of John the Blind.

"He fought alongside the Greeks, Alexander at Tyre and the Roman legionnaires. He was once a pirate, a cavalryman with Napoleon, and finally a tanker in the Great War," recalled World War II associate Col. Robert H. Nye, who knew Patton well. "He always suffered horrible deaths. God determined when he should return and fight again." For George Patton, there could be no greater glory than to die in battle. That fate eluded him.

———◦———

"Courage is fear holding on a minute longer."

———◦———

"If we take the generally accepted definition of bravery as a quality which knows not fear, I have never seen a brave man. All men are frightened. The more intelligent they are the more they are frightened.

"The courageous man is the man who forces himself, in spite of his fear, to carry on. Discipline, pride, self-respect, self-confidence and the love of glory are attributes which will make a man courageous even if he is afraid." ~ *Journal entry.*

———◦———

"Accept the challenges so that you can feel the exhilaration of victory."

———◦———

"All men are timid on entering any fight. Whether it is the first or the last fight, all of us are timid. Cowards are those who let their timidity get the better of their manhood." ~ *Patton in a letter to his son at West Point, June 1944.*

———◦———

"At Saarlautern, I crossed the bridge over the river under alleged fire. It was purely a motion on my part to show the soldiers that generals could get shot at. I was not shot at very much." ~ *Journal entry, November 8 to December 8, 1944.*

———◦———

"I drove to Trier via Wasservillig. The Roman Legions

marching on Trier from Luxembourg used this same road and one could almost smell the coppery sweat and see the low dust clouds where those stark fighters moved forward into battle. As a memorial to their great deeds, the least demolished building standing in Trier was the gateway to the Roman amphitheater." ~ *Journal entry, January 29 to March 12, 1945.*

"The crossing of the three divisions of these rivers [the Our and Sauer rivers] was a magnificent feat of arms. The rivers were in flood to such an extent that the barbed wire along the Siegfried Line, which abutted on the rivers, was under water, and, when the men disembarked from the boats, they were caught in it. The whole hillside was covered with German pillboxes and barbed wire. A civilian observer told me afterward that he did not see how human beings could be brave enough to succeed in such an attack." ~ *Journal entry, February 7, 1945.*

"You are not all going to die. Only two percent of you right here today would die in a major battle. Death must not be feared." ~ *Patton to various units of the Third Army in England, March to May 1944.*

"The 10th Armored Division was in Trier and had captured a bridge over the Moselle intact. This . . . was due to the heroic act of Lieutenant Colonel J.J. Richardson, deceased. He was riding in the leading vehicle of his battalion of armored infantry when he saw the wires leading to the demolition charges at the far end of the bridge. Jumping out of the vehicle, he raced across the bridge under heavy fire and cut the wires. The acid test of battle brings out the pure metal." ~ *Journal entry, January 29 to March 12, 1945.*

"The light feelings of love and reverence for our country engendered by shouting for the flag on the 4th of July are too haphazard, too cheap. The man who has served a year with sweat and some discomfort feels that truly he has a part in his country, and that of a truth he has, and he is a patriot."

———

"There is a time to take counsel of your fears and there is a time to never listen to any fear."

Chapter 14

Poems of Sorrow

In 1919, during the final days of the Great War, Patton wrote to his wife about an incident when some of his men encountered a German gun emplacement:

"One of my tanks was attacking a machine gun when the gun in the tank jammed so the men decided to run down the machine gun. The two [Germans] fired to the last and the tank went over them. Next day they were found still holding their gun, though dead. There could be nothing finer in war. My men buried them and put up crosses."

In battle Patton would destroy his enemies. In death, he knew they deserved a final tribute . . . a salute to the brave.

A Soldier's Burial
(1919)

Not midst the chanting of the Requiem Hymn,
    Not with the solemn ritual of prayer,
        'Neath misty shadows from the oriel glass,
            and dreamy perfume of the incensed air was
                he interred;

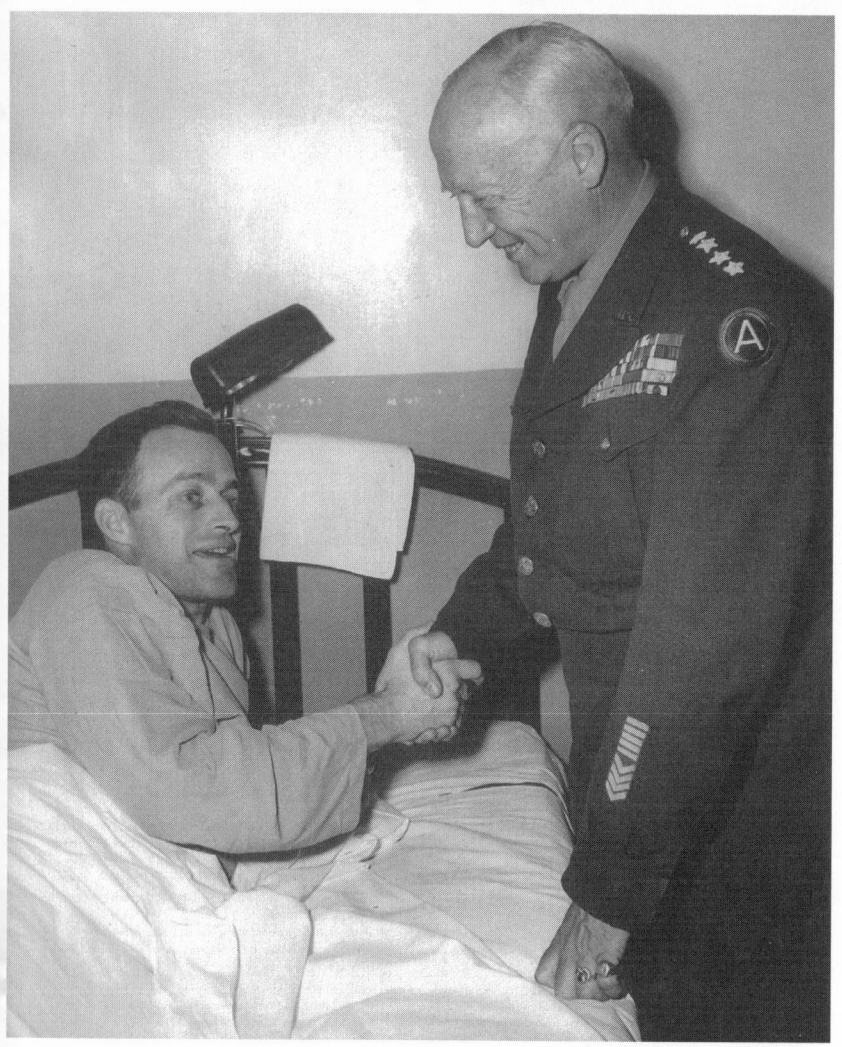

Perceived to be tough as nails and spitting fire, General Patton in fact hated the deaths of "his boys" in combat. He frequently visited military cemeteries and field hospitals, mourning the carnage of war. He rarely showed his feelings in public, but in his writings, in his very personal poetry, Patton revealed his compassionate side. After the surrender of Nazi Germany, Patton enjoyed a victory tour of the States in mid-1945. While in Washington, D.C., he visited Walter Reed Hospital, where his son-in-law, Lt. Col. John K. Waters, was recuperating after being held for three years in a German POW camp. Waters had been captured during the Tunisian campaign and was finally freed in 1945, when Patton ordered soldiers from his Third Army to liberate the camp. (National Archives)

But in the subtle stillness after fight,
   and the half light between the night and the day,
      We dragged his body all besmeared with mud,
         and dropped it, clod-like, back into the clay.

Yet who shall say that he was not content,
   Or missed the prayers, or drone of chanting choir,
      He who had heard all day the Battle Hymn
         Sung on all sides by a thousand throats of fire.

What painted glass can lovelier shadows cast
   Than those the evening skies shall ever shed,
      While, mingled with their light, Red Battle's Sun
        Completes in magic colors o'er our dead
         The flag for which they died.

———

Wars begin when diplomacy fails and then it becomes a conflict of man against man. The weaponry becomes more lethal from one decade to the next, but it is still man inflicting his will on his enemies, while loved ones at home wait, hopeful but helpless.

George Patton was one who directed the battles and developed the advances in weaponry between the Great War and World War II. His poems reveal the psyche of a complex Spartan warrior.

This poem, based on his experiences in World War I, with trench warfare and poison gas, personifies the moon as a woman looking down on the battlefield still littered with the dead and wounded.

The Moon and the Dead
(1918)

The road of the battle languished,
   The hate from the guns was still,

While the moon rose up
    from a smoke cloud,
        and looked at the dead on the hill.

Pale was her face with anguish,
    Wet were her eyes with tears,
        As she gazed on the twisted corpses,
            Cut off in their earliest years.

Some were bit by the bullet,
    Some were kissed by the steel,
        Some were crushed by the cannon,
            But all were still, how still!

The smoke wreaths hung in the hollows,
    The blood stink rose in the air;
        and the moon looked down in pity,
            At the poor dead lying there.

Light of their childhood's wonder,
    Moon of their puppy love,
        Goal of their first ambition,
            She watched them from above.

Yet not with regret she mourned them,
    Fair slain on the field of strife,
        Fools only lament the hero,
            Who gives for faith his life.

She sighed for the lives extinguished,
    She wept for the loves that grieve,
        But she glowed with pride on seeing,
            That manhood still doth live.

The moon sailed on contented,
   Above the heaps of slain,
      For she saw that manhood liveth,
     and honor breathes again.

To Our First Dead
(1918)

They died for France like countless thousands more
   Who, in this war, have faltered not to go
At duty's bidding, even unto death.
   and yet, no deaths which history records,

Were fought with greater consequence than theirs.
   A nation shuddered as their spirits passed;
and unborn babies trembled in the womb,
   In sympathetic anguish at their fate.

Far from their homes and in ungainful strife
   They gave their all, in that they gave their life;
While their young blood, shed in this distant land,
   Shall be more potent than the dragon's teeth

To raise up soldiers to avenge their fall.
   Men talked of sacrifice, but there was none;
Death found them unafraid and free to come
   Before their God. In righteous battle slain

A joyous privilege theirs; the first to go
   In that their going doomed to certain wrath
A thousand foemen, for each drop they gave
   Of sacramental crimson, to the cause.

And so their youthful forms all dank and stiff,
   All stained with tramplings in unlovely mud,

We laid to rest beneath the soil of France
    So often honored with the hero slain;

Yet never greatlier so than on this day,
    When we interred our first dead in her heart.
There let them rest, wrapped in her verdant arms,
    Their task well done. Now, from the smoke veiled sky,
They watch our khaki legions pass to certain victory,
    Because of them who showed us how to die.

In Memoriam
(1918)

The war is over and we pass to pleasure after pain
    Except those few who ne'er shall see their native land again.
To one of these my memory turns noblest of the noble slain
    To Captain English of the Tanks, who never shall return.

Yet should some future war exact of me the final debt
    My fondest hope would be to tread the path which he has set.
For faithful unto God and man and to his country true
    He died to live forever in the hearts of those he knew.

Death found in him no faltering, but faithful to the last
    He smiled into the face of Fate and mocked it as he passed.
No, death to him was not defeat, but victory sublime
    The grave promoted him to be a hero for all time.

Dead Pals
(1919)

Dickey, we've trained and fit and died,
    Yes, drilled and drunk and bled,
        and shared our chuck and our bunks in life.
            Why part us now we're dead?

Would I rot so nice away from you,
    Who has been my pal for a year?
        Will Gabriel's trumpet waken me,
            If you ain't there to hear?

Will a parcel of bones in a wooden box
    Remind my Ma of me?
        Or isn't it better for her to think
            Of the kid I used to be?

It's true some preacher will get much class
    A tellin' what guys we've been,
        So, the fact that we're not sleeping with pals,
            Won't cut no ice for him.

They'll yell, "Hurrah!"
    and every spring they'll decorate our tomb,
        But we'll be absent at the spot
            We sought, and found, our doom.

The flags and flowers won't bother us,
    Our free souls will be far—
        Holdin' the line in sunny France
            Where we died to win the war.

Fact is, we need no flowers and flags
    For each peasant will tell his son,
        "Them graves on the hill is the graves of
            Yanks, Who died to lick the Hun."

And instead of comin' every spring
    To squeeze a languid tear,
        A friendly people's loving care
            Will guard us all the year.

"The Life and Death of Colonel Gasenoyl" is a tribute to two of General Patton's fellow officers from the Great War, Col. Harry Semmes and Col. Harry "Paddy" Flint, who both distinguished themselves under fire.

Colonel Semmes was in the thick of the fighting, leading an armor unit against Vichy French forces in North Africa, when his tank was hit several times. He promptly used his anti-tank gun to return the favor and blasted four enemy tanks.

Paddy Flint did not have armored protection when he confronted Nazi forces at Troina on Sicily. He boldly stood rock solid, stripped to the waist and smoking a cigarette, daring the enemy troops to take their best shot, while his own soldiers questioned his sanity. He called out, "Shoot, you bastards! You can't hit me." The Nazi soldiers certainly did their best to accommodate him, but all they did was inspire Flint's own soldiers to advance on the enemy and send them to the hereafter or a POW camp for the duration of the war. A year later, Flint was shot in the head at close range. General Patton lost a dear friend and wrote the poem as a tribute.

The Life and Death of Colonel Gasenoyl
(Excerpt, 1944)

In Nineteen Hundred and forty-four
    Our land was swept by cruel war
Such parlous times, these halting rhymes
    Can only indicate, no more.

As usual our land defense
    had been cut down to save expense
To a squad or two, which even you'll admit
    is not much armaments.

This paltry force was much despised,
    but the enemy was soon surprised.
For the Cavalry was a sight to see.
    This Cavalry was mechanized!

The soldiers loved old Colonel G.
    No greater man, they thought, than he.
But a soldier's fate was now in wait
    For that mechanical S.O.B.

Oh! What a horrid scene was there,
    Where once had been so brave and fair
Oil and blood were mixed like mud.
    The fumes of gas were everywhere.

But the saddest sight of all to see
    Was the pitiful plight of Colonel G.
A wounded Titan, through with fightin'
    His dying words were, "God d— me!"

George Patton was undeniably brash, arrogant, pompous, and headstrong. But he was the one Allied commander that the German High Command feared the most. From North Africa to Sicily—shown here at Gela, on July 11, 1943—then on to France and Northern Europe and finally over the Rhine into Germany, Patton's Army could not be stopped. (U.S. Army)

Chapter 15

On Patton

George Patton had numerous influences, rooted in the centuries-old tales of bold leaders whose legacies are etched in stone:

"He was very clear in recognizing what was necessary to be done, even when it was a matter still unnoticed by others; and very successful in conjecturing from the observation of facts what was likely to occur. In marshalling, arming and ruling an army he was exceedingly skillful; and very renowned for rousing the courage of his soldiers, filling them with hopes of success, and dispelling their fear in the midst of danger by his own freedom of fear." (Arrian, writing about Alexander the Great)

"So great were the good-will and devotion of Caesar's soldiers to him, that those who under other generals were in no way superior to ordinary soldiers, were invincible and irresistible and ready to meet any danger for Caesar's glory." (Plutarch, writing about Caesar)

Centuries later, those same comments could be applied to George Patton.

Studying many of the great commanders in history, he felt that a leader should be at the front with his unit, exposed to the same dangers as his troops. Near Cheppy in World War

I, he led his tank battalion up a hill, where they were pinned down by enemy machinegun fire. "I felt a great desire to run, I was trembling with fear when suddenly I thought of my progenitors and seemed to see them in a cloud over the German lines looking at me. I became calm at once and saying aloud, 'It is time for another Patton to die,' called for volunteers and went forward to what I honestly believed to be certain death," Patton later wrote. Still under fire and wounded in the skirmish, he remained to coordinate the Allied attack until he was evacuated and patched up. There were many more instances in the two world wars when Patton was exposed to danger yet refused to pull back out of harm's way.

———✦———

"In the summer of 1918, a group of soldiers of the 301st Tank Brigade, which I commanded, was having 37mm gun practice which I was observing. One defective round exploded in the muzzle, wounding two or three men. The next round exploded in the breech, blowing off the head of the gunner. The men were reluctant to fire the next round, so it was incumbent on me, as the senior officer present, to do so. In fact, I fired three rounds without incident. This restored the confidence of the men in the weapon. I must admit that I have never in my life been more reluctant to pull a trigger."

———✦———

"I still get scared under fire. I guess I never will get used to it, but I still poke along."

———✦———

"I am scared, but I still want to get to the front."

———✦———

"I have trained myself so that usually I can keep right on talking when an explosion occurs quite close. I take a sly pleasure in seeing others bat their eyes or look around."

———

"When I was a little boy at home, I used to wear a wooden sword and say to myself, 'George S. Patton Jr., Lieutenant General.' At that time I did not know there were full generals. Now I want, and will get, four stars." ~ *Patton after getting his third star and taking over II Corps in March 1943.*

———

Getting that fourth star was not enough for George Patton. He wanted to be revered as one of the greatest commanders of epic battles. He disliked the moniker "Old Blood and Guts," but he was also referred to as "Flash Gordon" and "the Green Hornet." Of course, there were a few other choice nicknames said behind his back, but what he liked to hear the most was simply, "Sir."

Patton was always immaculately dressed, whether striding with purpose across a smoldering battlefield or riding in his staff car, sometimes standing, or sitting upright and rigid, "like Washington crossing the Delaware," recalled author John P. Marquand. "He had a sentimental streak. He wanted his men to admire him as much as he admired himself. And furthermore, God d— it, he wanted to be loved!"

———

"People ask why I swagger and swear, wear flashy uniforms and sometimes two pistols. Well, I'm not sure whether or not some of it isn't my own fault. However that may be, the press and others have built a picture of me. So, now, no matter how tired, or discouraged, or really even ill I may be, if I don't live up to that picture, my men are going to say, 'The old man's sick, the old son of a bitch has had it.' Then their own confidence, their own morale will take a big drop."

———

"All the men steal looks at me . . . it is complimentary but a little terrible. I am their God or so they seem to think."

"I believe that one's spirit enlarges with responsibility and that, with God's help, I shall make [momentous decisions] and make them right. When this job is done, I presume I will be pointed to the next step in the ladder of destiny. If I do my full duty, the rest will take care of itself." ~ *Journal entry during the North Africa campaign, November 6, 1942.*

"On the opposite of the road was an endless line of ambulances bringing men back; wounded men. Yet, when the soldiers of the 90th Division saw me, they stood up and cheered. It was the most moving experience of my life and the knowledge of what the ambulances contained made it still more poignant." ~ *Journal entry, December 19, 1944, to January 28, 1945.*

"As usual on the verge of action, everyone felt full of doubt except myself. It has always been my unfortunate role to be the ray of sunshine and the backslapper before action, both for those under me and also those over me." ~ *Journal entry, December 19, 1944, to January 28, 1945.*

"There must be one commander for ground, air and sea. The trouble is we lack leaders with sufficient strength of character. I could do it and possibly will. As I gain experience, I do not think more of myself, but less of others. Men, even so called great men, are wonderfully weak and timid. They are too damned polite. War is simple, direct, and ruthless. It takes a simple, direct and ruthless man to wage it." ~ *Journal entry, April 15, 1943.*

"I wish to assure all of my officers and soldiers that I have never and will never criticize them for having done too much.

However, I shall certainly relieve them for doing nothing."

"Sometimes I think that I am not such a great commander after all; just a fighting animal."

"They all get scared and then I appear and they feel better."
~ *Patton to his wife, Beatrice, September 1, 1944.*

"May God have mercy upon my enemies, because I won't."

"I continued to walk up and down the beachhead and soon shamed them into getting up and fighting."

"Leadership is the thing that wins battles. I have it, but I'll be damned if I can define it. It probably consists of knowing what you want to do and then doing it and getting mad as hell if anyone tries to get in your way. Self confidence and leadership are twin brothers."

Some of Patton's contemporaries thought he made decisions too quickly, on the fly. Meanwhile, he viewed their indecision and lengthy deliberations as a simple lack of brass balls! They never understood that Patton studied his opponent, analyzed the battlefield and planned for contingencies well in advance, and considered countermoves for when things didn't go just right. What may have appeared to others as hasty and haphazard reactions were actually well-thought-out maneuvers to seize the enemy by the throat and dispatch them to the hereafter!

"Whether these tactical thoughts of mine are the result of

inspiration or insomnia, I have never been able to determine, but nearly every tactical idea I had ever had has come into my head full-born, much after the manner of Minerva from the head of Jupiter." ~ *Journal entry, January 29 to March 12, 1945.*

———

"Papa always told me that the first thing was to be a good soldier. Next was to be a good scholar."

———

"I'm a hell of a guy. I'm giving the men hell one minute and crying over them the next."

———

"War is the only place where a man lives."

———

"I visited the troops near Coutances and found an armored division sitting on a road, while its headquarters, secreted behind an old church, was deeply engrossed in the study of maps. I asked why they had not crossed the Seine. They told me they were making a study of it at the moment, but could not find such a place and was informed that they were studying the map to that end.

"I then told them I had just waded across it, that it was not over two feet deep and that the only defense I knew about was one machine gun which had fired very inaccurately at me. I repeated the Japanese proverb—'One look is worth one hundred reports'—and asked them why in hell they had not gone down to the river personally." ~ *Journal entry, August 1 to September 24, 1944.*

———

Cold, callous, brutal, insensitive, vindictive . . . over the course of Patton's military service, those were just some of the harsher terms others used to describe him. Maybe he did have a crusty exterior, but he also had a soft spot few ever saw or knew of.

During a conversation with Henry J. Taylor from the Scripps-Howard newspapers in mid-March of 1945, on the eve of the assault on the Rhine River, Patton said, "Who do you suppose knows what it means to order an attack and know that in a few hours thousands of our boys are going to be killed or hurt? War is my work and I know I sound sometimes as though I liked it; perhaps I do, but this war hurts everybody and at times like this I wish I could just fight single-handed, alone."

"One man had the top of his head blown off and they were just waiting for him to die. He was a horrid bloody mess and was not good to look at or I might develop personal feelings about sending men into battle. That would be fatal for a general."

"It's God awful. It's terrible, that's what it is. I can see it in a vision. It comes to haunt me at night. I am standing there knee deep in the water and all around me as far as the eye can see are dead men, floating like a school of dynamited fish. They are all floating face up with their eyes wide open and their skins a ghastly white. They are looking at me as they float by and they are saying, 'Patton, you bastard, it's your fault. You did this to me. You killed me.' I can't stand it, I tell you."

"Godd—it, I'm not running for the Shah of Persia. There are no practice games in life. It's eat or be eaten, kill or be killed. I want my bunch to be in there first, to be the 'firstest with the mostest.'"

With the defeat of Nazi Germany in April of 1945, George Patton was ready to head to the far side of the world with his victorious Third Army and take on Imperial Japan. But there

wasn't room for two enormous egos in the Pacific Theater—
Dauntless Doug MacArthur and George Patton.

According to Col. Henry C. McLean, "It does not take great
penetration to observe that MacArthur does not want Patton
to come to the Pacific. He does not want anyone who will steal
the limelight or any of the glory from him. It would be very
easy to do, as Patton has plenty of color and appeal which
MacArthur lacks."

Instead, Patton returned to a hero's welcome in Boston,
in June of 1945, decked out in all his finery. After another
ovation in Los Angeles, he returned to Germany to become
military governor of Bavaria, though he wasn't exactly sure
what the future had in store.

"If we let Germany and the German people be completely
disintegrated and starved, they will certainly fall for
Communism and the fall of Germany for Communism will
write the epitaph of Democracy in the United States."

———

"Someone must win the war and also the peace."

———

"Peace is going to be a hell of a letdown."

———

"His life was the stride of a demi-god, from battle to battle
and from victory to victory," wrote J. W. von Goethe, on
Napoleon Bonaparte.

"What distinguishes [him] the most is not his skill in
maneuvering, but his audacity. He carried out things I never
dared to do," stated Napoleon about Frederick the Great. The
remarks about both of these revered leaders could also refer
to George Patton, who truly believed he was destined to create
a lasting legacy as a great warrior, one who would be studied
and critiqued and talked about for generations to come.

Chapter 16

Farewell

George Patton was a learned man, a student of warfare, who could recite verbatim lengthy passages from those leaders who inspired him to greatness. One such leader was Alexander the Great, who said, "Whoever of you has wounds, let him strip and show them, and I will show mine in turn; for there is no part of my body . . . remaining free from wounds, nor is there any kind of weapon used either for close combat or for hurling at the enemy, the traces of which I do not bear on my person. For I have been wounded with the sword in close fight, I have been shot with arrows and I have been hit with missiles projected from engines of war, and though of ten times I have been hit with stones and bolts of wood for the sake of your lives, your glory and your wealth, I am still leading you as conquerors over all the land and sea, all rivers, mountains and plains."

Titus Livius wrote on Hannibal:

"There was no leader in whom the soldiers placed more confidence or under whom they showed more daring. He was fearless in exposing himself to danger and perfectly self-possessed in the presence of danger. He was by far the foremost both of the cavalry and the infantry, the first to enter the fight and the last to leave the field."

After Hitler's Thousand-Year Reich was destroyed, General Patton was charged with rebuilding Bavaria, in southern Germany. As with many units from the European campaign, Patton's could have been sent to the Pacific, for the final push to defeat Imperial Japan. But after a brief victory tour of the States, Patton returned to Germany with little to do. In December 1945, his vehicle was involved in a minor traffic accident, but it left Patton paralyzed. He died less than two weeks later. It was not the warrior's death he had always hoped for. (Patton Museum)

He could have easily been writing many years later about Patton. No commander drove his troops harder than Patton, but no leader cared more for them either. And while many senior officers made their tactical decisions far from the front lines, a safe distance from danger, Patton prowled the combat zone regularly. He felt it was the best way to assess the rapid movements in war and redirect the offensive as needed.

"Death, in time, comes to all men. Yes, every man is scared in his first battle. If he says he's not, he's a liar. Some men are cowards but they fight the same as the brave men or they get the hell slammed out of them watching men fight who are just as scared as they are. The real hero is the man who fights even though he is scared. Some men get over their fright in a minute under fire. For some, it takes an hour. For some, it takes days. But a real man will never let his fear of death overpower his honor, his sense of duty to his country and his innate manhood.

"Battle is the most magnificent competition in which a human being can indulge. It brings out all that is best and it removes all that is base." ~ *Patton to various units of the Third Army in England, March to May 1944.*

"It is foolish and wrong to mourn the men who died. Rather we should thank God that such men lived." ~ *Patton in Boston, June 1945.*

"There is one great thing that you men will all be able to say after this war is over and you are home once again. You may be thankful that twenty years from now when you are sitting by the fireplace with your grandson on your knee and he asks you what you did in the great World War II, you *won't* have to cough, shift him to the other knee and say, 'Well, your granddaddy shoveled s— in Louisiana." No, sir, you can look him straight in the eye and say, 'Son, your granddaddy rode with the Great Third Army and a son-of-a-Godd— bitch named Georgie Patton!'" ~ *Patton to various units of the Sixth Armored Division in England, May 31, 1944.*

———

Around 1900, Patton's father taught him that, according to Viking folklore, the true heroes were those who died in battle. Before every armed conflict, the Valkyrie selected the Norse warriors who were worthy of a valiant death. The "chosen ones" could look forward to the afterlife, in Valhalla.

Many years later, after victory in North Africa, Patton was attending a Medal of Honor ceremony when he was heard to say, "I'd love to get that medal . . . posthumously."

———

"The only way for a soldier to die is by the last bullet of the last battle of his last war."

———

Patton wanted nothing more than to die in battle, violently, valiantly. Instead, after returning from a day of pheasant hunting in Bavaria, he was involved in a minor traffic accident, on the ninth of December in 1945. Though there was little damage to his staff car, Patton had sustained a broken neck and was paralyzed. He held on for twelve days, finally giving up the fight on the twenty-first. (Some conspiracy theorists believe that Patton was killed while lying helpless in his hospital room.)

He was buried at the military cemetery at Hamm in Luxembourg, alongside several thousand of his Third Army soldiers. The greatest battlefield commander of World War II's European campaign had rejoined his boys, his valiant heroes.

May all their ever-afters be peaceful ones.

Bibliography

Allen, Robert S. *Lucky Forward.* New York: Vanguard, 1947.

Ambrose, Stephen. "A Fateful Friendship." *American Heritage* (April 1969).

Army Times. Famous American Military Leaders of World War II. New York: Dodd, Mead, 1962.

———. *Warrior: The Story of General George S. Patton.* New York: GP Putnam's Sons, 1967.

Ausubel, Nathan, ed. *Voices of History, 1945-46.* New York: Gramercy, 1946.

Ayer, Frederick. *Before the Colors Fade: Portrait of a Soldier. George S. Patton.* Boston: Houghton Mifflin, 1964.

Baldwin, Hanson W. *Battles Lost and Won.* New York: Konecky and Konecky, 1966.

Bloomfield, Gary L. *Duty, Honor, Victory. America's Athletes in World War II.* Guilford, CT: Lyons, 2003.

Blumenson, Martin. "George S. Patton: Extraordinary Leader; Extraordinary Man." In *John Biggs Cincinnati Lectures in Military Leadership and Command.* Lexington, VA: Virginia Military Institute Foundation, 1987.

———. "The Many Faces of George S. Patton, Jr." Paper presented at the U.S. Air Force Academy, Colorado Springs, CO, 1972.

———. *The Patton Papers.* Boston: Houghton Mifflin, 1974.

———. "Patton the Soldier." *Ordnance* 43 (January-February 1959).

Brinkley, Douglas. *The World War II Desk Reference.* New York: Grand Central, 2004.

Carroll, Andrew. "A Sidelined General Shares His Philosophy on Leadership." *World War II* (July 2009).

Charton, James, ed. *The Military Quotation Book.* New York: St. Martin's, 1990.

Collier, Richard. *Fighting Words. The War Correspondents of World War Two.* New York: St. Martin's, 1989.

D'Este, Carlo. *Patton: A Genius for War.* New York: HarperCollins, 1995.

Devaney, John. *Blood and Guts.* New York: Julian Messner, 1982.

Dietrich, Steve E. "The Professional Reading of General George S. Patton Jr." *Journal of Military History* (October 1989).

Essame, H. *Patton—A Study in Command.* New York: Charles Scribner's Sons, 1974.

Farago, Ladislas. *The Last Days of Patton.* New York: McGraw Hill, 1980.

———. *Patton: Ordeal and Triumph.* New York: Ivan Obolensky, 1963.

Finke, Blythe Foote. *General Patton: Fearless Military Leader.* Charlotteville, NY: SamHar, 1972.

Fisher, George. "The Boss of Lucky Forward." *Combat Forces Journal* 1 (May 1951).

Forty, George. *The Armies of George S. Patton.* London: Arms and Armour, 1996.

Frankel, Nat, and Larry Smith. *Patton's Best.* New York: Hawthorn, 1978.

Gavin, James M. "Two Fighting Generals: Patton and MacArthur." *Army* (April 1965).

Green, Michael. *Patton's Tank Drive: D-Day to Victory.* Osceola, WI: Motorbooks International, 1995.

127

Hackworth, David. "Bring Back Blood-and-Guts Patton." *Parameters* (September 1987).

Hastings, Max. *Overlord: D-Day and the Battle for Normandy.* New York: Simon and Schuster, 1984.

Hatch, Alden. *George Patton: General in Spurs.* New York: Julian Messner, 1950.

Hirshson, Stanley P. *General Patton. A Soldier's Life.* New York: HarperCollins, 2002.

Hogg, Ian V. *The Biography of General George S. Patton.* New York: Gallery Books, 1982.

Irving, David. *The War Between the Generals.* New York: Congdon and Lattes, 1981.

Leopold, Christopher. *Blood and Guts Is Going Nuts.* New York: Doubleday, 1976.

MacDonald, Charles B. *A Time for Trumpets: The Untold Story of the Battle of the Bulge.* New York: Morrow, 1985.

Mellor, William. *Patton, Fighting Man.* New York: Putnam, 1946.

Nye, Roger H. *The Patton Mind: The Professional Development of an Extraordinary Leader.* Garden City, NY: Avery, 1993.

O'Neill, James H. "True Story of the Patton Prayer." *Review of the News* (October 6, 1971).

Patton, George S., Jr. Papers. Henry E. Huntington Library, San Marino, CA.

———. Papers. Manuscript Division. Library of Congress.

———. Papers. Special Collections of the U.S. Military Academy, West Point, New York.

———. Papers. United States Army Military History Institute, Carlisle Barracks, PA.

———. "Success in War." *Cavalry Journal* (January 1931).

———. *War as I Knew It.* Boston: Houghton Mifflin, 1947.

Pearl, Jack. *Blood and Guts Patton: The Swashbuckling Life Story of America's Most Daring and Controversial General.* Derby, CO: Monarch, 1961.

Pfannes, Charles E., and Victor A. Salamone. *The Great Commanders of World War II: The Americans.* Zebra Books, 1981.

Polk, James H. "Patton: 'You Might as Well Die a Hero.'" *Army* (December 1975).

Porch, Douglas. *The Path to Victory.* New York: Farrar, Straus and Giroux, 2004.

Prioli, Carmine, ed. *Lines of Fire: The Poems of General George S. Patton Jr.* Lewiston, NY: Edwin Mellen, 1991.

Province, Charles M. *The Patton Principles.* San Diego: CMP, 1978.

———. *Patton's One Minute Messages: Tactical Leadership Skills for Business Managers.* Novato, CA: Presidio, 1995.

Puryear, Edgar F., Jr. *19 Stars. A Study in Military Character and Leadership.* Novato, CA: Presidio, 1971.

Robichon, Jacques. *The Second D-Day.* New York: Walker, 1962.

Semmes, Harry. *Portrait of Patton.* New York: Paperback Library, 1955.

Stillman, Richard J. *General Patton's Timeless Leadership Principles.* New Orleans: Stillman, 1997.

Strobridge, Truman. "Old Blood and Guts and the Desert Fox." *Military Review* (June 1984).

Weigley, Russell. *Eisenhower's Lieutenants.* Bloomington: Indiana University Press, 1981.

Whiting, Charles. *Patton.* New York: Ballantine Books, 1970.

Zabecki, David T. "The Untold Story of Patton at Bastogne." *World War II* (November 2007).